KEEP OUT!

Build Your Own Backyard Clubhouse
A STEP-BY-STEP GUIDE

Lee Mothes

Storey Publishing

*To Mom, Chris, Kathy, and Virginia, for enabling me
to find my way by building clubhouses.*

*The mission of Storey Publishing is to serve our customers by
publishing practical information that encourages
personal independence in harmony with the environment.*

Edited by Deborah Balmuth and Nancy Ringer
Art direction and book design by Alethea Morrison
Text production by Liseann Karandisecky

Photography and ephemera courtesy of: Lee Mothes, 6 and 10–14; Michele Brodie Basile, 8 and 9; Images from the Past, Bennington VT, 75; Jack Presbury, 88 and 89; Everett Caldwell, 103; Carolyn Miller, 133; John P. Rickerhauser, 146; David Lindemulder, 175; Merrall MacNeille, 206 and 207; Don Cook, 217
Cover and interior color illustrations by © Peter Oumanski
Plan drawings and how-to illustrations by Lee Mothes

Indexed by Catherine Goddard

Storey Publishing
210 MASS MoCA Way
North Adams, MA 01247
www.storey.com

Printed in the United States by Versa Press
10 9 8 7 6 5 4 3 2 1

Library of Congress Cataloging-in-Publication Data on file

CONTENTS

Part 1
GETTING READY TO BUILD, 16

Part 2
BUILDING A CLASSIC CLUBHOUSE, 50

Part 3
THE ADVANCED CLUBHOUSE
Building a Backyard Hideaway, 134

PREFACE

MY CLUBHOUSE BUILDING ADVENTURES

My greatest feeling of accomplishment as a kid occurred after school one day when I sat in a beat-up wicker chair outside our clubhouse. We — two girls and two boys — had just finished nailing up shingles that we had scrounged from a building site and hauled home on a wagon. I was beaming with pride at what we had achieved. After all, we designed and built the entire structure ourselves from stuff we found on our own, without a single suggestion or intervention from grown-ups.

The clubhouse was our hangout, where we learned to work together and to tolerate the sometimes strange habits of other kids. We had no choice but to get along: some kids provided the wood, nails, and paint, another's parents owned the yard, and I had figured out how to build it. We had arguments and breakdowns, but our common desire to have a clubhouse kept us together. I think that because we had the freedom to get dirty, learn how to use our hands, and make mistakes on our own, we all had more fun building clubhouses than anything we ever did under the supervision of adults.

Discovering Clubhouses

I was probably a mediocre kid — a bit of a loner in my elementary school, not interested in sports, and my reading habits favored comic books. But I was fascinated by building things. My mom had told me about her brother Frank, who was the only boy in her otherwise strictly disciplined family of girls. Frank, at age 13, built his own little "house" on a vacant lot across the street. Mom praised her brother's ingenuity, and I found myself hooked; I wanted a clubhouse too!

At about this time, my grandfather Jesse gave me a weatherworn set of Audels Carpenters and Builders Guides, published in 1923. These books contained everything known about building houses, at least in 1923. I pored over the hundreds of detailed drawings of foundations, floors, walls, roofs, dormers, stoops, and stairs, paging through them as I did my comic books. I saw building as an intricate puzzle and felt challenged to figure out how all the pieces were put together to make a house. Maybe I could do something like this. . . .

Herein the mysteries of house building were revealed to me.

Study hall at school was my favorite time to draw plans. The floor plan on the right included an early patio.

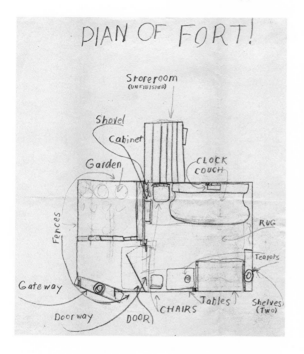

Starting to Build

My best friend Chris and I had formed a bond by building things together. We spent hours on our nearby beach building sand castles, sand houses, sand towns, and sand freeways with elaborate bridges. The beach offered a trove of washed-up building materials and other treasures, scattered among the seaweed and dead seagulls. We spent hours on end doing this, but after a while, we wanted to build something bigger.

At age 11, I felt I was ready to build a clubhouse of my own, and Chris was eager to help. We chose a sandy vacant lot near my house as our building site. By luck, a late winter storm had washed up a lot of junk on the beach, including some usable lumber, and our next-door neighbor had just thrown out a pile of tall plywood cabinet doors. Chris and I lugged the doors, the driftwood, and any other wood we could scrounge up to our site. With my mom's hammer and handsaw and all the nails I could find in our garage, we went to work. However, we had little idea of how to transform the pile of wood in front of us into a clubhouse; for all my studying of the pictures in Audels, the complexities of house building were still a bit beyond us.

So we improvised by sinking four 2×4 corner posts into the sand (easy digging, luckily), nailing the long 1×6 boards to these, and then shorter boards to the longer boards, until all the walls and the roof were covered with wood, except where the door would be. I nailed a door together with more boards and used rubber sandal soles for hinges. We managed to finish our clubhouse, a wobbly box about 7 feet long by 7 feet wide and 5 feet high, in about a week. A friendly neighbor heard about our project and donated a picket fence for a little front yard.

Learning Social Realities

This clubhouse became quite a learning experience! For fun, I put up a "No Girls Allowed" sign next to the door, but we soon found out that having the girls on our side would be a much better idea. Chris's sister Chele, her friend Kathy, and Kathy's older sister Jean (who was bigger than me) took offense at the sign. They delivered a warning note that said "Take down the sign OR ELSE!!!!!!" We ignored it. Then they showed up with a wagonload of stones, which they hurled at the clubhouse without mercy, trapping us inside until they proved their point. Finally, after a long assault, Jean hollered, "Hey, we'll stop if you take that sign down." I yelled back, "Okay!" and I took it down. We

Chris and his sister Chele, before the battle, in front of our first clubhouse.

all knew each other and had played together before, so after the battle we became better friends.

I also found out what can happen to a clubhouse if it is left unattended, especially on a vacant lot. One day a neighbor kid I didn't especially like cheerfully admitted he had blown up an old clock we had in the clubhouse with a cherry bomb. Ha ha! Later, someone stole my mom's hammer, and then one morning Chris and I found the clubhouse had been totally wrecked. He cried, and I almost did, too!

While we were without a clubhouse, we found that Kathy and Chele were great fun to play with. After a summer of bike riding and hiking expeditions (mostly Kathy's idea), we decided to build a clubhouse for the four of us. Kathy's family happened to have the perfect site: an unused and somewhat junky space in their backyard, surrounded by a six-foot fence. But getting permission wasn't easy. We waited in suspense while Kathy pleaded with her parents to let us build . . . and finally Kathy's mom, Virginia, took a chance on trusting us not to make a bigger mess or kill ourselves!

MAR • 60

Hanging out after school

The four of us found more lumber, nails, a window, and hinges for a door, and eventually we built a clubhouse large enough for all of us to comfortably fit in at once. We also managed to find old wallpaper, a shelf, a chair, and other goodies, mostly by rummaging through the neighbors' trash, for decoration. With more help from my Audels Guides, I learned how to build a real floor, solid walls, and a roof that wouldn't leak! We painted the whole thing turquoise. We were very proud and also amazed at how bright it was!

The outside became equally domesticated. We laid down old bricks for a walk and built a tiny patio in front of the clubhouse. I brought in drought-hardy geranium and succulent cuttings from my mom's overgrown front yard, as well as nasturtium seeds, and even a little tree that had sprouted in our yard. This all added to our amazement that we — a bunch of unsupervised kids — could build all this and grow plants too.

Things Fall Apart, and Then We Build Again

When I turned 13, I suddenly went from feeling happy one day to sad, then mad, all without really knowing why. Tired of comic books and TV, I retreated into my shell and moped around a lot, feeling bored. My friends didn't seem to be around much, either, and we didn't use the clubhouse as frequently.

Then one day I thought of building a hideaway place all my own. I had no lumber, so I tore down most of the clubhouse in order to build my own "fort" in a narrow, dark space behind our garage. It was tiny, secretive, and not much fun to play in all by myself, so I wound up storing my bike in it. Kathy, her mom, my mom, Chris, and Chele were all upset when they discovered I had torn down the clubhouse. I lamely argued that some of the wood was mine and that I needed it, but inside I felt they were right. I should not have wrecked the clubhouse.

After a while, something, perhaps loneliness or a desire to make good, prompted me to suggest to Kathy that maybe I should rebuild the old clubhouse. Kathy immediately said, "Yes!" and her mom said, "Okay, but don't you dare tear it down again." I humbly agreed.

We did it again and better! The proud builder has just completed another paint job.

THE CLUBHOUSE

A new club member named Russell joined us, and Chele moved on to other interests, so we formed a new club and rebuilt our clubhouse better than ever. We found two nice windows this time, built another back room, and planted more plants. At school, when I should have been studying, I drew more plans and then pictures of the clubhouse — I couldn't stop!

In the four years we had our clubhouses, we loved to gather in them to talk, gossip, eat snacks, and read comic books away from the eyes, ears, and demands of grown-ups. Chris, Kathy, and I also spent a lot of time rearranging furniture, painting some part of the clubhouse (again), digging, planting, or sweeping the brickwork outside. We didn't think of ourselves as little housekeepers; it was just fun to do.

Like most clubs, we wrote down rules, sometimes conducted meetings, and on occasion collected dues, usually for junk food. Some of the moments of our club were recorded in our Club Diary (I was known as Rusty, or Big Rusty, while our new member Russell was called "Little Rusty" or "Mustard").

Finally, in 1964, our clubhouse-building days came to a close. Our members scattered or became interested in other things. The clubhouse remained where it stood, surprisingly intact, for another 50 years, a memorial to the good times we shared there together.

The clubhouse still stands today.

RULES OF THE CLUB

1. NO GUESTS ALLOWED IN THE CLUBHOUSE UNLESS 2 HONORARY MEMBERS ACCOMPANY THEM.

2. <u>NO ONE</u> ALLOWED ON THE ROOF, INCLUDING MEMBERS. (UNLESS IT HAS TO BE REPAIRED)

3. THERE IS A 10 CENT-A-WEEK DUES FOR ALL MEMBERS. WHEN A SPECIAL THING IS TO BE BOUGHT THE DUES ARE 20¢ A WEEK. /STARTING JAN. 1, 2064

4. The time limit for being kicked out, is 20 years, 3 months, 18 days, 7 hours, 3 mins, and exactly 46½ seconds. The penalty for breaking this rule, is <u>Death</u>! (So don't forget!)

5. IF ANYTHING IS DONATED BY A CLUB MEMBER (FULL OR HALF MEMBER) AND IS BUILT INTO THE CLUBHOUSE OR CLUB YARD, THE MEMBER CANNOT TAKE IT OUT AGAIN, EVEN IF HE GETS KICKED OUT OF THE CLUB.

6. <u>NO</u> FEET OR HANDS ON THE WALLS, CEILING OR SHELVES

7.

Club Diary

March 30, 1963: Today Rusty came to Sunset Beach from Seal Beach onhis bike. He met Rusty (Mustard), came to the Clubhouse, and decided to build the shelves. Big Rusty asked Kathy for some good wood, and she got it. Then he started building it, and Kathy helped. It was pretty hard, because the boards kept on splitting. They finally finished and it looked pretty good. Mustard came back from H.B., with a hair cut, and some tennis shoes. A Siamese cat came into the clubhouse, and lost half of its hair. Big Rusty also brought a Club Seal. It is really neat lookin'. After Big Rusty and Kathy were done building the shelves, they had a lemonaide and potatoe chip party. Mustard didn't get any lemonaide, hahaha so we had share ours with him. (Darn). Chris didn't come over at all today, but Chele, came over looking for him, and said he was gunna get killed. Adle called, but Kathy side-tracked her.

Respectfully Submitted
by Your Club Secretary,
Kathy Strain ✳

INTRODUCTION
WHY BUILD A CLUBHOUSE?

There's not much that's more rewarding than building your very own shelter, with your own two hands. It can be a rough structure that the kids use as a clubhouse or a more polished construction for the whole family to use as a backyard getaway. You — yes, you, no matter what your age — can build it with just a few inexpensive hand tools, basic building supplies, and some simple building skills, which this book will teach you. All you need is some enthusiasm, a few helpers, and a bit of ingenuity to make it your own.

There's nothing like a place of your own . . .

Clubhouses have enjoyed a timeless mystique, and for good reason. Here kids enjoy a bit of independence, develop social skills, and cultivate friendships. When I was a kid, my friends and I were lucky enough to experience the deep satisfaction of hanging out inside a sturdy shelter that we had built ourselves. The real pleasure came from the fact that with our own hands we created a place we could proudly call our own, and we did it together.

However, in recent years it has become more difficult for kids to build things on their own. Out of fear, mistrust, or social pressure, parents have been less inclined to let their children do anything creative outside without adult supervision. Meanwhile, electronic games, online social media, and ever-pervasive television give kids more reasons not to play outside at all.

The solution? Build a clubhouse! Building an outdoor shelter can be a wonderful learning experience for kids and grown-ups alike. Whenever kids use their own creativity to accomplish something, they learn on a deep and permanent level. By building a clubhouse, they not only gain a valuable skill but also create a private space of their own that they can be proud of. The dirt, scratches, banged thumbs, and other difficulties they encounter along the way only increase the value of this endeavor. Because it's their own project, kids have fun doing it, and that is the key: When there is passion and enjoyment, amazing things can happen.

When parents build with their kids, the same things can happen. If the grown-ups have never built anything before, then they learn along with the kids — and the excitement is mutual. Grown-ups (or parents) who want their own clubhouse can easily build a slightly bigger shelter, with all the comforts of a tiny home or cabin: safe, strong, weather-resistant, and as decorated as they'd like it to be.

In this book, I'll share with you everything I've learned about building clubhouses and small shelters. I've included adaptable plans and techniques to enable you to build whatever size, shape, or style of structure you'd like. And for more inspiration, I'll share the stories of several other clubhouse builders throughout.

Whatever your age, treat this project as a journey, and forget about whether you can do it or not. This is a guide to help you create what you want, to make something real with your own hands, and to experience something you'll never forget. Whether you're 10, 12, or 82, you'll find the building of a clubhouse to be a compelling adventure and wonderfully satisfying achievement.

Part 1

GETTING READY TO BUILD

Wouldn't you love to have a place of your own where you can gather your friends, talk privately, build models, write in a journal, draw, paint, read, think, sleep, or just spend time?

Whether you're a kid or a grown-up, if you have the desire, you can build an outdoor clubhouse (or any other kind of permanent retreat). It's no big mystery, and I'll show you how. The biggest challenge might be to convince those around you, such as parents or spouses, to believe that not only can you do this but that a clubhouse will benefit them as well.

Clubhouse designs range widely. Much will depend on the materials you find and on your own ideas. Simple is good, especially in the beginning. The best way to start out is by building a one-room clubhouse, as described in chapters 3–5. To this, you can add a room, a garden patio, or maybe a second story. You can also add interior walls (partitions) and do all kinds of

things to the inside and outside to make it as comfortable or as crazy as you'd like.

In the following chapters, I will introduce you to the essential tools you'll need to build your clubhouse, show you how to find the materials for it, and help you figure out a design. Then I will take you through all the steps to actually build your clubhouse. If you want to finish the structure with class, you'll find details on that, too.

But first, here are a few ideas for the great ways you can modify your clubhouse to make it one-of-a-kind.

The Classic Clubhouse

The Classic Clubhouse is a simple, good-size clubhouse for most kids. I'll explain how to build this clubhouse in part 2.

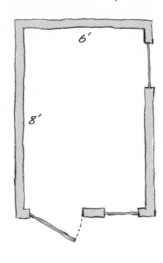

Many variations are possible. The doors and windows can go in different places, and you can decorate it however you want, inside and out!

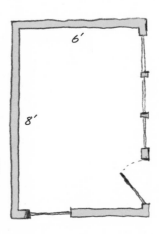

The Clubhouse with a Patio

This is how your clubhouse might look with a patio and a trellis built out of some 2×4s, 2×2s, two posts, and split-bamboo fencing or old bamboo blinds. (See chapter 7 for details on building a patio and trellis.)

The El

This is a Classic Clubhouse with a room added, and the door and windows in different places. (See chapter 6 for details on building a room addition.)

6'

5'

original
room

el   5'

8'

The Clubhouse of Many Rooms

If you have the space and your friends or family members all want to have a hideaway or room of their own, this is possible. On the original clubhouse, you can add rooms to the outside as you need to. In one of them, you can build a secret escape hatch. You might also have space inside to add a partition. Just remember to build the added roofs with a slant so they don't leak.

original room 6' x 8'

The Fun-with-Doors Clubhouse

If you can find about six to ten solid-wood doors (not hollow core or particleboard core), you can use them to build a unique clubhouse. Salvage yards sometimes sell old doors quite cheaply. Doors with glass in them can also be used as windows. With a clubhouse made of doors, your friends can be the only ones who know which one actually opens.

The Weird Stuff Clubhouse

People have built actual houses with bottles, cans, tires, newspaper (mixed with cement), cordwood, straw bales, and canvas. Others have used old boats, shipping pallets, and shipping containers. There is at least one house out there covered with license plates and another with a porch shingled with phonograph records. I once saw an entire floor built with old plywood road signs, which county highway departments sometimes throw out. With a little imagination, you can use any of these materials for your clubhouse instead of buying all new stuff.

The Pile

A clubhouse can evolve into something much different from your original design. The materials you find and location you wind up with can challenge your flexibility, and that can be a good thing: The result can be truly original.

It's best to start with a plan, but it's okay to change that plan if you find six old doors or you simply get a new idea. It can be challenging to change your design to fit something you found, so relax and take your time. This is a clubhouse and it's all right to make mistakes.

CHAPTER 1

TOOLS AND TECHNIQUES

A clubhouse is essentially made of wood and nails, and a few common hand tools are all that are needed to build one. In this chapter, I'll show you how to use these tools. For more experienced builders or grown-ups, I'll add a few make-life-easier tools, including some basic power tools.

If you've never done any building before, be patient as you learn how to hit nails and saw boards. You're learning with your body as well as with your mind, and, as with dancing, tennis, or snowboarding, that takes a while. Once you learn the basics, you'll find it relatively easy to master other carpentry tools and to build bigger or more complex clubhouses.

The Nine Essential Tools

The first thing you'll need before building anything is your own set of simple, good-quality hand tools. Believe it or not, you can build an entire house with the nine essential tools listed here. Do everything you can to get your own set.

1. **A 16-ounce claw hammer.** This is a "finish hammer," which is lighter than a "framing hammer" and just right for young builders. A wooden-handled hammer is fine, but a fiberglass-handled one will last longer.

claw hammer

2. **A 15-inch-long handsaw,** often called a "toolbox saw." Stanley makes good ones, and I don't have to tell you they are very sharp.

handsaw

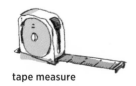

tape measure

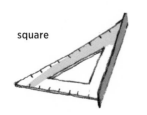

square

pencil

screwdriver

level

crowbar

sawhorse

3. A tape measure. A 12- or 16-foot-long tape is easy to handle for young builders, while a 20- to 25-foot-long tape is more suitable for grown-ups.

4. A 7-inch rafter or speed square. Use this for marking boards to make accurate saw cuts. Although shaped like a triangle, it's called a *square* because it has two sides that make a right angle, which defines a square in geometry. Later, I'll show you how to use the marks on this kind of rafter square to cut boards at angles.

5. An ordinary pencil. You'll use a pencil for marking boards.

6. Screwdrivers. You can get a Phillips screwdriver (which has a cross-shaped slot) and a standard straight-slot screwdriver, or you can get a combination screwdriver with interchangeable blades. The combination-style screwdrivers include a set of smaller blades, but they have one drawback: The little snap-in blades can easily get lost. Make sure the blades or tips are made of hardened steel; cheap ones wear out fast.

7. A level. Look for a 9-inch-long plastic "torpedo" level. These are quite accurate and can fit in any toolbox.

8. A crowbar. You'll need this to remove nails and pull apart mistakes. I like the Stanley Wonder Bar or a similar flat bar bent to this shape.

9. Sawhorses. Sawhorses make building much safer and easier. The plastic fold-up kind are sturdy and a good height for grown-ups with power saws. Lower sawhorses are better for hand-sawing and for younger builders. You can build your own sawhorses with some common boards and these essential tools. As a practice project, I'll show you how to build them later in this chapter.

One more sort-of-tool: A nail pouch or nail apron to hold a tape measure, pencil, and nails will be useful. Lumberyards sometimes give these away.

Safety Means Taking It Slowly

Before you begin, take a deep breath and relax. Building *always* takes longer than you think, especially if this is your first project. Nails get bent, saws cut crooked, thumbs get whacked, and splinters get under your skin. Most of these annoyances and injuries are the result of not focusing or trying to do something too fast.

Here are a few things to remember about safety:

- Focus only on sawing when you saw a board. Find a friend to help hold the board down, or use clamps, and saw slowly. Stop sawing if you want to talk.

- The same thing applies when you pound in nails: Focus only on the nail and where your hands are.

- Don't leave nails sticking out of boards! Pound them back through, pull them out, or bend them over flat. Some barefoot kid is bound to come around and step on the one board in the whole yard that has that nail sticking out. A screaming injured child can kill a clubhouse project faster than you can say, "Oops." This also applies to nails that are poking through the inside of your clubhouse walls.

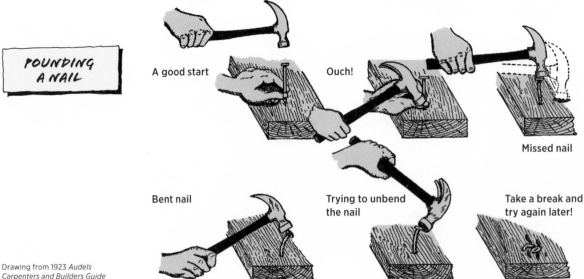

POUNDING A NAIL

A good start   Ouch!   Missed nail

Bent nail   Trying to unbend the nail   Take a break and try again later!

Drawing from 1923 *Audels Carpenters and Builders Guide*

- Wear gloves if you are handling recycled or rough-sawn lumber. Old wood dries out over time and can get splintery.

- For you grown-up builders: Wear goggles and a dust mask when you're using a power saw. Also, unplug power tools even if you are going away for only a few minutes.

How to Pound a Nail, Measure, and Saw a Board

Before you get started on your first building project, you'll want to practice pounding nails, using a tape measure, and cutting a board. Think of this as batting practice.

Pounding Nails

You've probably pounded a few nails in the past, but pretend you're doing it for the first time. Get your hammer, a few large nails, and a long, thick board like a 2×4, and get comfortable.

If you are right-handed, hold the nail with your left hand and the hammer with your right. If you are left-handed, do the opposite. Hold the hammer handle at the far end, away from the hammerhead, and tap the nail into the wood hard enough so it stands up on its own. Then move your nail-holding hand away and drive in the nail. The drawings on the facing page show the right way to start and what can happen if you miss. Just keep trying.

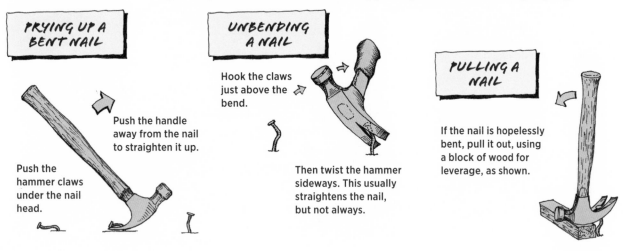

PRYING UP A BENT NAIL

Push the handle away from the nail to straighten it up.

Push the hammer claws under the nail head.

UNBENDING A NAIL

Hook the claws just above the bend.

Then twist the hammer sideways. This usually straightens the nail, but not always.

PULLING A NAIL

If the nail is hopelessly bent, pull it out, using a block of wood for leverage, as shown.

Measuring a Board for Cutting

To measure a board, you'll need a tape measure, pencil, and square. Wear your tool belt or nail apron to hold the tape measure and pencil.

A tape measure has all those numbers and little marks that show feet, inches, and fractions of inches. Some tape measures also show centimeters and meters, but we'll only use inches here. The numbers tell you the feet and inches, and the little marks show the fractions of an inch. Each inch is divided into fractions of an inch, including halves, quarters, eighths, and sixteenths.

Get a board from your lumber pile, say, a 2×4. To find out its exact dimensions, hook your tape measure across the wide part of the 2×4. You'll see that the board is actually 3½″ wide. (Why isn't a 2×4 actually 2″ by 4″? See the box on the facing page.) Next, measure the board's thickness; you should get 1½″. As you build with these boards, you'll be using these actual dimensions in your planning.

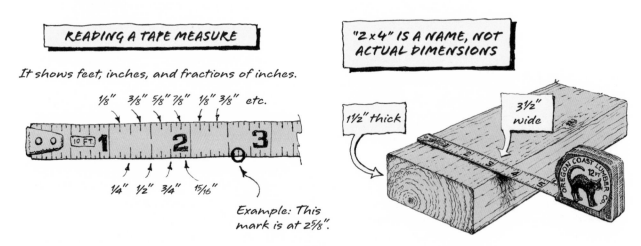

READING A TAPE MEASURE

It shows feet, inches, and fractions of inches.

⅛″ ⅜″ ⅝″ ⅞″ ⅛″ ⅜″ etc.

¼″ ½″ ¾″ ¹⁵⁄₁₆″

Example: This mark is at 2⅝″.

"2×4" IS A NAME, NOT ACTUAL DIMENSIONS

1½″ thick

3½″ wide

Now let's mark the board to prepare it for cutting. Say you need some 6-foot-long 2×4s to support your floorboards (which you will), and you have 8-foot-long 2×4s in your pile. Put one of these 2×4s on your sawhorses (or chairs or a bench until you build your sawhorses). Hook the tape measure at one end, and pull the tape down the board until you reach 72″, which is 6 feet. The tape measure might say "6F" there, too, which also means 6 feet.

Using your pencil, make a mark on your board next to that mark on the tape measure, right between the 7 and the 2 in 72. Then set your square on the board, with its wide, or flanged, edge pulled tight against the bottom of the board. Set the square's other edge to your mark, and draw a *cut line* over your mark with your pencil, as shown below.

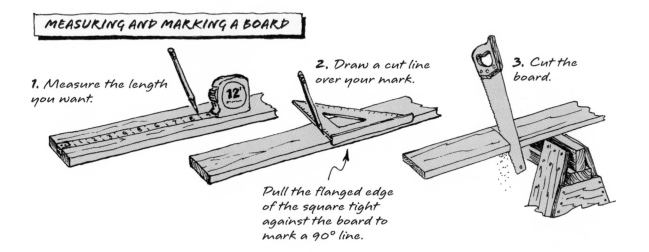

MEASURING AND MARKING A BOARD

1. Measure the length you want.

2. Draw a cut line over your mark.

3. Cut the board.

Pull the flanged edge of the square tight against the board to mark a 90° line.

Why a 2×4 Isn't Really 2″ by 4″

At the lumber mill, logs are rough-sawn into boards that are 1″ or 2″ thick and from 2″ to 12″ wide. (The symbol ″ means "inches.") The rough boards are then sur-faced with a planer, which in the process of smoothing them makes them smaller. Therefore, a so-called 2×4 might have started out at 2″ thick and 4″ wide (its nomi-nal size), but it has been planed down to 1½″ thick and 3½″ wide (its actual size).

Older salvaged or unplaned boards might be closer to their nominal dimensions. Try measuring different boards to see what you get.

Sawing a Board

Now that your board has been measured, get your saw and sawhorses if you have them. (To build your own sawhorses, see facing page.) To start, see the drawing below to figure out how to hold down the board. You can have a friend help hold the board for you, or use clamps if you have them.

When cutting, use a sharp saw! Start by setting the teeth of the saw at the cut line, then pull up the saw to start the cut (see the drawing below). Saw with long, slow strokes. Leaning over your board as you work, push and pull the saw along the line you drew. You'll find that the push strokes do most of the cutting. If the saw wanders off the line, back up and slowly, patiently resaw toward the line. After a while, you'll be able to saw on the line you're following with ease. When you get near the end, saw the last stroke fast so the scrap falls off without taking a splintery piece of your good wood with it. In the meantime, it's okay if the cut is off the line a little; don't worry, this is still batting practice.

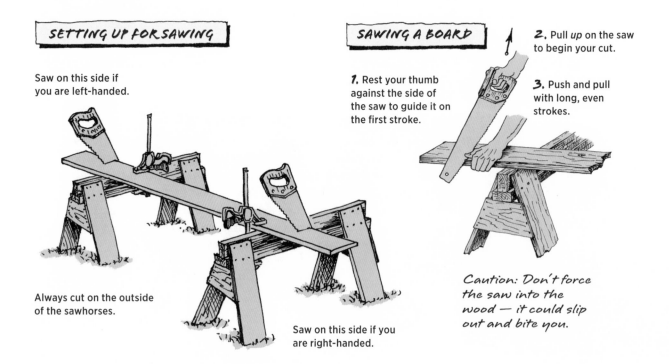

SETTING UP FOR SAWING

Saw on this side if you are left-handed.

Always cut on the outside of the sawhorses.

Saw on this side if you are right-handed.

SAWING A BOARD

1. Rest your thumb against the side of the saw to guide it on the first stroke.

2. Pull *up* on the saw to begin your cut.

3. Push and pull with long, even strokes.

Caution: Don't force the saw into the wood — it could slip out and bite you.

HOW TO BUILD YOUR OWN SAWHORSES

Now you're ready to build your sawhorses, right? This will be good practice, and when they are completed, you'll be glad you have them.

Find some old chairs or a bench or something to cut wood on. You will need some 2×4 and 1×6 boards, some scraps of ½″-thick plywood, and nails. Have your tape measure, pencil, saw, square, and hammer handy. Here is a list of what to gather up or buy to make two sawhorses:

Sawhorse Materials

Quantity	Description
2	2×4s, 6 feet long
2	1×6s, 8 feet long
1	2 × 4-foot panel ½″-thick plywood (or one 1×6, 4 feet long)
1 pound	6d coated sinkers or galvanized box nails
1 pound	8d coated sinkers or galvanized box nails
1 pound	12d or 16d coated sinkers or galvanized box nails

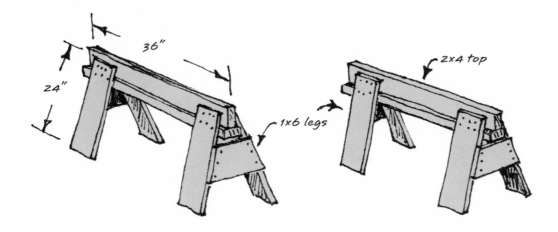

HOMEMADE SAWHORSES

36″

24″

2×4 top

1×6 legs

Step 1. For the sawhorse tops, cut four pieces of
2×4 that are each 36" long. To do this, measure to 36"
from the end of each 2×4 with your tape measure.
Mark the spot with your pencil, then use your square
to draw a cut line at the mark. Saw along the cut line
with a sharp handsaw.

Step 2. Find a hard floor or concrete surface on
which to nail these together. Nail the 2×4s together
with 12d or 16d nails, as shown in the drawing at
right. Use four or five nails for each pair.

Step 3. For the legs, measure and saw eight 24"-
long pieces from your 1×6 boards. Nail these to the
2×4 tops, using five or six 8d nails per leg.

Step 4. For the braces, hold a 1×6 board or a small
piece of plywood against the end of the sawhorse,
as shown at right. Draw lines where this board (the
brace) covers the legs, then saw off the extra wood.
Using three or four 6d nails per leg, nail the braces to
the legs.

There, you did it! It probably took a while and
you might have bent some nails, but this was
good practice and also kind of a test. If you *really*
hated every part of doing this, then now is the
time to decide whether you really want to build
your own clubhouse. On the other hand, if you
feel good about having done this, even though
a board split open and you banged your thumb
twice, then by all means keep building.

Don't worry if you miss, just keep pounding.

STEP 2: NAIL THE TOPS TOGETHER

STEP 3: NAIL THE LEGS TO THE TOPS

about 1"

STEP 4: PUT ON THE BRACES

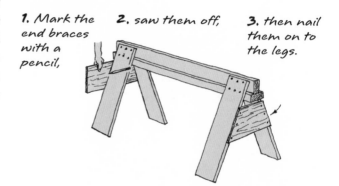

1. Mark the end braces with a pencil, **2.** saw them off, **3.** then nail them on to the legs.

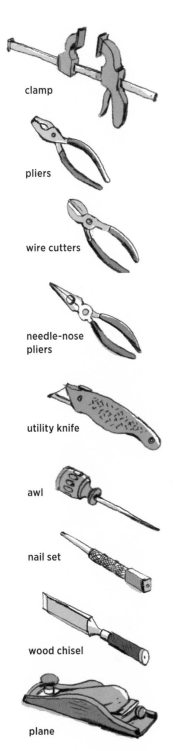

clamp

pliers

wire cutters

needle-nose
pliers

utility knife

awl

nail set

wood chisel

plane

Make-Life-Easier Tools

As you get used to using your nine essential tools, you'll eventually feel the need for more tools to make building easier and safer. These tools will also be useful to help put siding, roofing, and trim boards on your clubhouse.

- **Clamps.** If you feel your board is wiggling too much when you're sawing and all of your friends went home, you might want clamps to hold it down. Clamps are also great for gluing and other assembly. The new lightweight quick-grip clamps are much easier to use than the traditional iron C-clamps. I recommend a set of two 12″ clamps or two 6″ clamps.

- **Pliers and wire cutters.** A basic set includes standard pliers, wire-cutting pliers (great for biting off small nails that won't pry out), and needle-nose pliers for all sorts of uses.

- **A utility knife with a retractable blade.** Use this knife for cutting tar paper or shingles for your roof, making cut lines for cleaner saw cuts, or shaving wood too thin for a saw to cut off. Be careful — the blade is sharp!

- **An awl or scratch awl.** This is used for poking pilot holes for screws or for scratching a cut line if you don't have a pencil. An awl is also handy to hold the end of a tape measure to a piece of wood.

- **A nail set.** To sink nail heads into the wood, use a nail set, which you hit with a hammer. A medium size with a $\frac{3}{32}$″-wide point is good for most needs.

- **A $\frac{3}{4}$″-wide wood chisel.** The steel cap on the chisel allows you to hit it with a hammer, which is necessary for most chiseling. Watch for nails when chiseling — the hardened-steel blade will chip easily.

- **A small hand plane or block plane.** Planes are helpful for shaving wood, especially when fitting windows and doors. Make sure you don't hit any nail heads while using the plane . . . very bad for the blade.

sanding block

toolbox

stepladder

- **A sanding block and sandpaper sheets.** Use these for knocking off splinters and smoothing wood before painting. Get 100-grit or medium-grit sandpaper to start with. Grit size is roughly the number of sand grains per inch. The lower the number, the bigger the grains. Sandpaper at 400 grit is very smooth, while 50 grit is rough.

- **A toolbox.** You'll want one that is at least 19″ long to put all your gear in.

- **A longer level or a straight board.** Once you start building bigger floors and higher walls, you'll want a longer level. An alternate trick is to attach your torpedo level to a straight 6 foot long or 8-foot-long 2×4 with rubber bands. Cut notches into the board where the rubber bands are placed so the board rests flat while you are leveling.

- **A 6-foot stepladder.** Someone probably has one you can borrow.

- **Plumb bob and layout line.** A plumb bob is a great tool for finding out whether something is "plumb," or straight up and down. Layout line, sometimes called mason's line, is strong white or colored string that usually comes on a handy plastic spool. These tools are both used to lay out a foundation on bare ground. An 8-ounce brass plumb bob is best. To make it work, attach a 9-foot-long piece of the layout line inside the removable top of the plumb bob.

- **Chalk line.** A chalk line is a long string coated with blue or red chalk that is used to make long saw-cut lines or guide lines, such as when nailing shingles on a wall. The line is kept in a chalk box that you fill with powdered chalk from time to time.

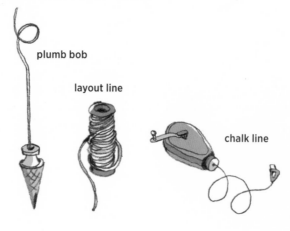

plumb bob

layout line

chalk line

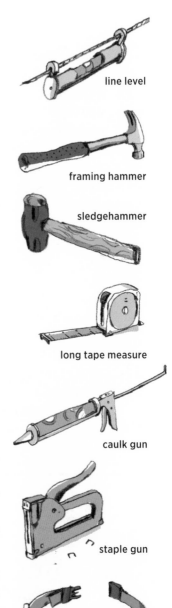

line level

framing hammer

sledgehammer

long tape measure

caulk gun

staple gun

tool belt

- **Line level.** This 3″-long level is designed to hang on a tightly stretched layout line. It will give you an accurate-enough reading for leveling a small shelter foundation.

- **Framing hammer.** A framing hammer is relatively heavy (at 20 or 22 ounces), which makes it easier to pound in all those 12d or 16d nails. Get one with a smooth face, rather than a waffle face; a waffle head chews up the wood (and your hand) if you miss.

- **Sledgehammer.** Get one with a 3- to 6-pound head to drive in stakes and for other blunt pounding chores. Choose the heaviest you feel you can comfortably swing.

- **Long, wide tape measure.** If you're building a large clubhouse or shelter, you'll want a longer tape measure, in the range of 20 to 25 feet long. Get one with a ¾″- or 1″-wide blade, which can be extended farther without bending.

- **Caulk gun.** This "gun" holds a variety of construction adhesives used for gluing sheathing panels to the shelter frame, as well as caulk for sealing narrow gaps between siding and windows. To use it, put a tube of caulk in the barrel, trim off or open the tip, then squeeze the trigger until the stuff starts coming out. To stop it, you sometimes have to loosen the plunger away from the tube of caulk.

- **Medium-duty staple gun.** This will come in handy when you are putting up plastic vapor barriers, roofing underlayment (tar paper), and insulation. Try out different models to find one that feels comfortable. Some heavy-duty staple guns require a powerful grip to staple and can get tiresome.

- **Tool belt.** A carpenter's tool belt certainly makes life easier. The best "system" I know of consists of a nylon web belt, a couple of bags, and a steel hammer loop. One bag is for nails and the other is for small tools such as your square, tape measure, pencil, chisel, and so on. Buy the bags, loop, and belt separately, and then adjust their positions to your liking.

Power Tools for Grown-ups

Once you have practiced with the hand tools that you've acquired, you'll likely want to get a few power tools to save time. A portable circular saw, a power drill, and a jigsaw or saber saw are all you really need.

circular saw

A portable power circular saw can be intimidating at first. It's loud, it jerks when the motor starts up, and it has a sharp and fast-moving blade. But fear not — the saw is safe when handled properly. If you've never used one before, read the user's manual for your saw, especially the parts about how to hold the saw and how to adjust the blade for different board thicknesses. Also have someone experienced show you how to use it before you take over yourself.

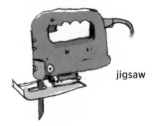

jigsaw

When using a power saw, always cut a board so the scrap falls off the end of your sawhorses, never between them, as shown below. If you cut the board between the sawhorses, it will pinch the blade and the saw might kick back at you. While cutting, push the saw gently and slowly across the board — let it do the work. The saw throws sawdust all over the place, so wear safety goggles.

power drill

Power drills are becoming more popular not only for drilling holes but also for assembling entire projects with construction screws instead of nails. A variable-speed reversible (VSR) drill works well as a power screwdriver.

A power jigsaw, reciprocating saw, or saber saw (all the same tool) is great for cutting out holes or making curved cuts on plywood panels or any wood up to 1½″ thick.

drill bits and drivers

For your power tools, get a heavy-duty electrical extension cord from 25 to 100 feet long, depending on how far your job is from the nearest outlet. Ask for a cord with 14-gauge or 12-gauge wire with a ground. A wimpy cord might damage the motors in your power tools. The ground is the third wire that protects you from electrical shocks if the tool gets wet or the cord is cut.

safety goggles

USING A CIRCULAR SAW

Clamp other end.

Set up the cut so that the scrap falls outside the sawhorse.

extension cord

CHAPTER 2
MAKING PLANS AND FINDING MATERIALS

You've assembled enough tools to get started, and now you are ready to make your clubhouse a reality. Next up is finding a building site and deciding how big you want your clubhouse to be. Then you'll get the materials.

Finding a Building Site

A fenced-in yard is usually the best location, but any out-of-the-way space will work. Front yards are made to look at, so you probably won't want to build there. A vacant lot or nearby woods might work, but there is a chance that someone will wreck it while you're away. A tucked-away corner in a backyard often works the best. If your summers are hot, try to find a shady spot.

Be careful not to choose a site too close to your neighbor's house. If there is no fence, talk to your neighbors about where the boundary is. (If there is a fence, don't use it as one of your walls.) Furthermore, don't build in front of someone's picture window or otherwise block their view. You will get complaints.

If you live in a community or subdivision that is heavily laden with owners' agreements or deed restrictions, check the rules to see if you can build in your yard. In recent years, some towns and homeowners' associations have ordered clubhouses removed because they are deemed unsafe, a fire hazard, unsightly, or all three. Many communities don't want to be "exposed to risk" from lawsuits or insurance claims. This unfortunate trend is part of the reason kids are no longer allowed to get outside, get dirty, and build clubhouses.

a likely clubhouse site

Kids ▶ Reality Check

As soon as a kid utters the word "clubhouse," parents or other Powers in Control will likely imagine a big mess to clean up. So here is where you'll need to think like a diplomat and argue your case like a lawyer.

Invite your parents to help decide on a good site for your clubhouse. If possible, have a second building site in mind so they have a choice. If that doesn't work, impress them with your knowledge of psychology: In recent years, children have been increasingly deprived of the outdoors and nature. Child-development specialists such as Richard Louv (author of *Last Child in the Woods*) have directly linked the absence of nature to the recent rise in obesity, attention disorders, and depression among children. Show them Louv's book or look up his website, and then ask them, "You don't want me to be overweight, have trouble learning, or get depressed, do you?"

Another good argument is this: "I'll be engaged in something creative, I'll be learning a lot of practical skills, and you will know where I am!" Then show them the plans you drew so they will know more about your project and that you are serious about doing it right. Tell them you'll follow the safety tips listed in chapter 1, and you'll keep the place as clean and neat as you can. Until they convince you it is impossible to build a clubhouse (you live in an apartment with no outdoor access, for example), keep trying!

If you're being told you can't build a clubhouse because of liability or "safety" concerns, try this idea, although it is a bit risky: Get your grown-up supporters to let you build a "protest clubhouse" and, if the Powers in Control demand its removal, offer to sign a "no fault" letter that promises you won't sue them or make a claim against their liability insurance. If *that* doesn't work, call in the local news media to make your point. This is America, after all. Good luck!

Drawing a Plan

Once you have a site, you can sketch out a plan. A plan, no matter how crude, works a lot better than just starting out nailing boards together. A plan is simply a way to think about what you want and how to get there. If you're a kid, a plan might also help you get permission and support for your project, so you might have to draw your plan *before* you start talking to the grown-ups. . . .

You can draw your plans freehand, you can use a ruler, or you can draw them on graph paper. On graph paper, for example, you can pretend each square is 3″, 6″, or 1 foot wide (you decide), and then count the squares. You

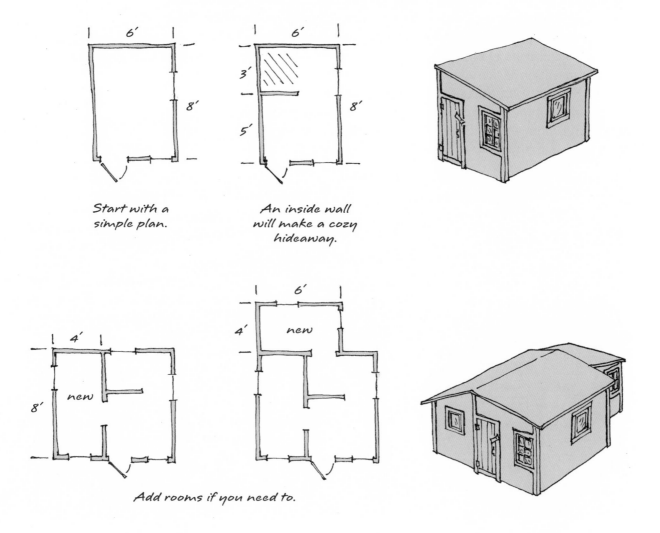

Start with a
simple plan.

An inside wall
will make a cozy
hideaway.

Add rooms if you need to.

can also pretend every inch or half-inch on a ruler is 1 foot on your plan. This way, you can figure out all the dimensions of your clubhouse, including the size of your windows and door. These methods are called drawing to scale, which I'll describe more thoroughly in chapter 2.

A floor plan is the easiest to draw. This will show you the floor of your clubhouse and the walls around it. First, see the box on facing page to help you plan your clubhouse. Then with a pencil, draw the walls as double lines. You can erase out spaces where you want your door, and make single lines where the windows will go. Change it around as many times as you want.

If you want to plan what your walls might look like, how your roof will slant, and where your windows will be, draw a side view, or elevation. This time, imagine how high off the floor the windows should be and which way the roof should slope. (Think about where you will want the rainwater to go.) Draw an elevation or side view for each wall, viewed from the outside. Again, you can draw it to scale using a ruler or graph paper.

By drawing plans, you can "see" how your clubhouse will look, how big it will be, and what will go where. Remember that plans are just ideas, so you can easily change them.

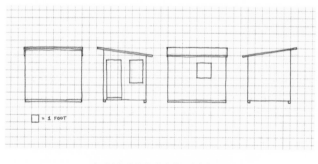

A SIMPLE ELEVATION

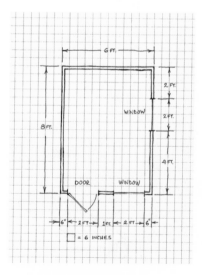

A SIMPLE FLOOR PLAN

Stuff to Think About

When planning your clubhouse, think about what you might want to do in it, and make a list: Will you want a desk or a couch? Will you want chairs or just cushions on the floor? Will you want a place to store or hide stuff, or a secret exit? Write these things down. Then think about how many people you might want in your clubhouse and how much space you'll need for them. For example, the Classic Clubhouse described in part 2 is 6 feet by 8 feet, which is enough to comfortably hold four people.

Next, check the site you've chosen to see if your clubhouse will fit. With your tape measure, check the actual size on the ground if you need to. You might have to make the clubhouse square-shaped or maybe 4 feet wide and 12 feet long to fit a tight space.

Also think about how you'd like to get in and out. What kind of door will you have, and where will it be? How much light and air do you want to let in? What kind of windows? Some people like their clubhouses dark and denlike, while others like a lot of light so they can read or see what's going on outside. Will you want a window to see who is approaching? A hinged window or two would be great for ventilation on hot days.

Think small, and plan to build one room at first. Later you can add more rooms (see chapter 6). Have fun!

Wood, Nails, and Carpenter Language

It's good to know what you'll need for your clubhouse so you can avoid collecting a lot of useless junk. Carpenters and lumberyards have their own words for the wood and other stuff they use or sell, and I'll explain these words as we go along. For example, a piece of framing lumber can be called a joist, a stud, a sill, a rafter, a trimmer, or a plate, depending mostly on where it is used. Nails are described by all sorts of names, such as roofing, drywall, duplex, casing, galvanized, coated sinker, box, or common, depending on their shape and where they are used. It's kind of like learning a new language, but you'll quickly catch on. These terms (and more) are defined in the glossary at the end of this book.

The rest of this chapter is devoted to helping you get familiar with the right materials and how much of them you will need. If you decide to build the Classic Clubhouse (described in part 2), use the materials list on page 53. If you want to build some other size or style of clubhouse, draw your own diagram similar to the one on facing page, then count the pieces of wood needed for the floor, the walls, and the roof. There are other estimating methods, but we'll keep it simple for now. As you count the pieces, make up a materials list like the one for the Classic Clubhouse. The list is an estimate, meaning you might have some extra pieces or you might have to get more stuff, especially if your plans change.

Note: Buying more than you need is generally a good idea. If you buy too many boards, you can return those you don't use. Lumberyards are nice about returns, especially if you return the boards in good condition (without any wood cut off them) and you bring your sales receipt with you.

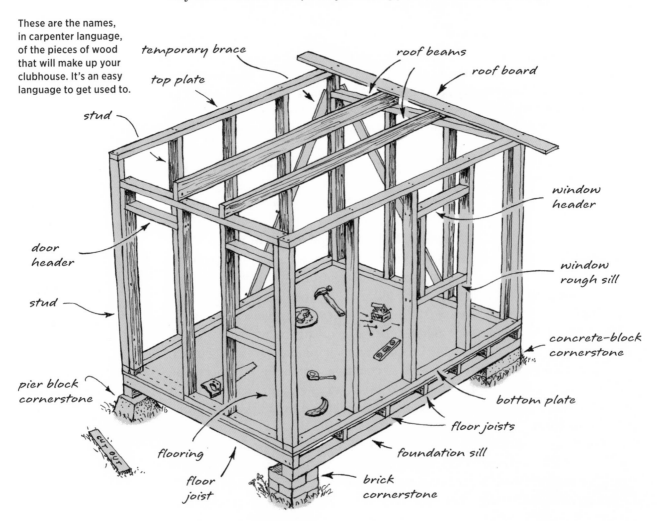

These are the names, in carpenter language, of the pieces of wood that will make up your clubhouse. It's an easy language to get used to.

temporary brace

top plate

roof beams

roof board

stud

window header

door header

window rough sill

stud

concrete-block cornerstone

pier block cornerstone

bottom plate

floor joists

foundation sill

flooring

brick cornerstone

floor joist

CUT OUT

Finding Materials

Now it's time to gather the wood, nails, and other materials you'll need for a strong clubhouse that will keep out the rain.

Recycled Materials

Use recycled materials if you can. Ask family, friends, and neighbors if they have any unwanted boards, windows, doors, bricks, shingles, roofing, siding, hinges, wallpaper, carpet, or paint. Cruise the streets and alleys in your neighborhood for cast-off materials on trash day. Ask permission before taking any materials, just to be sure. Salvaging the materials for your clubhouse can be a challenge, but it can be done. Besides saving money, you are also helping the planet.

Barn Windows and Other Salvage

If you can't find suitable recycled windows, some of the big lumberyards sell barn sash windows. These inexpensive four-pane or six-pane wood-frame windows are perfect for barns, sheds, and clubhouses.

You can also find recycled windows, doors, and boards at used building materials outlets. The Building Materials Reuse Association (www.bmra.org) lists stores and salvage yards that sell used building materials in every state in the US. You can also look in your local phone book yellow pages under "Building Materials — Used." The ReStore, operated by Habitat for Humanity, is a nationwide chain of recycled-materials stores. You might find one near you at www.habitat.org/restores. Goodwill and St. Vincent de Paul stores often sell inexpensive windows, doors, paint, carpet pieces, wallpaper, shelves, and other goodies with which to finish or furnish your clubhouse. Also, hardware-store paint departments sell returned custom-mixed paint at low prices. Just ask if they have any "returned custom-color" paint.

Kids ▶ Reality Check

No matter how much material you're able to scrounge from around your neighborhood, you will probably have to buy some of the lumber and the nails from a lumberyard, so you will need money and transportation. If you still need the basic tools listed on page 22, you'll need to shop for them as well. This brings up the topic of cooperation with grown-ups. If you offer to give them something they want, beyond what they already expect of you, there is a good chance you will get the materials and tools you will need, along with permission to build. In the process, you'll become good at real-world negotiating, a great lifetime skill.

Sometimes the materials you find might change your plan, so be flexible.

Foundation

For the clubhouse foundation, you'll need four cornerstones. These can be anything stonelike, such as large flat stones, concrete blocks, pavers, pier blocks, or bricks. Concrete retaining-wall blocks also work well. You can probably find enough of these around your neighborhood.

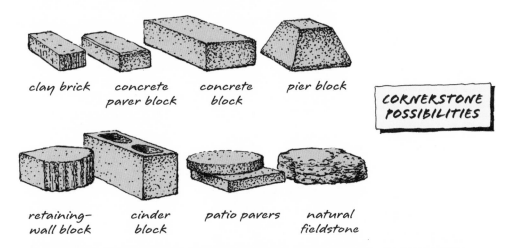

clay brick   concrete paver block   concrete block   pier block

CORNERSTONE POSSIBILITIES

retaining-wall block   cinder block   patio pavers   natural fieldstone

Evaluating Wood

It's okay to be picky and select the best boards out of the pile for your clubhouse. When choosing, here's what to watch out for:

- **BENT OR WARPED BOARDS.** Look down the length of the board as if you were aiming it like a rifle and see if it's curved or bent. You'll find that most boards are warped a little, so only put aside the ones that are *really* bent . . . you'll have to decide.
- **KNOTS AND CRACKS.** If there are big knots or knotholes (more than half the width of the board) or big cracks (called *checks*), put the board aside.
- **PITCH.** If you see yellowish sticky goo on a board, it is likely pine pitch. This stuff won't come off your hands or anything else, so set this board aside.

If you're at a lumberyard or home center and there aren't enough good boards to pick through, you can ask a salesperson to cut open one of the banded stacks, or units, behind the loose boards. Remember, it's their job to be nice to you. Once you've pulled out all the boards you want, be sure to restack the ones you've rejected.

Using 2×3s

Though 2×4s are most common and can sometimes be found (recycled) for free, if you have to buy lumber, you might think about using 2×3s to frame the walls. They are usually cheaper than 2×4s and are plenty strong enough, but they sometimes split and warp more than 2×4s. If you use 2×3s, remember that they are 1″ narrower (but just as thick) as 2×4s, which will affect the measurements of your walls. Don't use 2×3s for floors; they aren't strong enough.

Floor, Wall, and Roof Framing

For the skeleton or frame of your clubhouse, you'll need 2×4 boards. When they hold up your floor, they are called joists. If they are part of the walls, they are called studs.

At the big lumberyards and home centers, the framing lumber such as 2×4s and 2×6s is usually stacked in big piles on the floor. Every pile or stack has a sign describing the name of the board, such as "stud" or "standard board," the dimensions, and the price per piece of wood.

Studs, boards, and other lumber are usually labeled with a grade and the kind of tree they came from, such as hemlock, fir, or pine. Look for lumber that is graded no. 2 or better or that is labeled "stud grade." The lumber should specify that it has been kiln-dried; kiln-dried lumber won't shrink or warp as much as "green" or undried lumber. Most of the big lumberyards sell kiln-dried no. 2 and better framing lumber.

For our clubhouse frame, 6-foot-long 2×4s are the cheapest and long enough for most of the studs. If you can't find 6-footers, buy 7-foot or 8-foot studs.

These lumberyard signs tell you that this wood was dried in an oven or kiln and the grade is stamped or printed on each board. The signs also tell you the exact size of the boards as well as the price. "S4S" means that the board was planed or surfaced on all four sides. The term "whitewood" means any kind of pine or hemlock, and "KD" means "kiln-dried."

2×4×6′ stud
- kiln-dried
- grade stamped
- actual size 1½″×3½″

2×4×96 KD
Whitewood
Select Stud S4S

Cut Measurements:
1½″×3½″×96″

Some lumber is labeled "pressure-treated." This lumber has been treated with toxic chemicals to make it rot-resistant. You wouldn't want to use it in your clubhouse except for your 4×4 foundation sills, which are close to the ground and subject to moisture and insects. When you saw pressure-treated wood, wear a dust mask. Ordinary untreated wood will work fine for the rest of your clubhouse, as long as it's away from the soil.

One more thing: A big lumberyard often has a bargain area with "odd lots" or damaged piles of wood for sale at about half the normal cost. This material is usually special-ordered, slightly weathered, banged up, or otherwise unfit to be sold at the regular price. The bargain area might contain some fence boards, weird roofing, odd-colored decking, a whole pile of 1×4s for sale as a unit, or who knows what. If any of this stuff fits your list, snap it up. Most lumberyards also sell short lumber pieces or scraps up to 4 feet long. These are usually displayed in bins labeled "Value Wood." You can always use these shorter boards to fill small spaces while covering your walls, so pick through them to find some good ones.

Sheathing

For the outside skin of your clubhouse, you can use common boards, sheets of plywood, oriented strand board (OSB), or other thin lumber called sheathing.

"Common" or "standard" boards are 1×4, 1×6, or wider pine boards with some knots and other minor defects. "Premium," "select," or "clear" pine boards look nicer but are far more expensive. Lumberyards also sell boards called car siding, which are 1×6 or 1×8 pine boards that have tongue-and-groove edges (see the illustration below). These look attractive and are strong and cheap. Boards are easier to saw and put up one by one than the large plywood sheets. New boards can be more expensive, but remember that old fence boards, barn boards, shelf boards, or anything ¾" thick will work for clubhouse sheathing (see page 78).

COMMON BOARDS

1x3 furring strip | 1x4 porch flooring | 1x6 standard board | 1x8 car siding | 1x6 car siding | 1"-thick decking

If you have a friend to help you and a power saw, the most inexpensive panel sheathing is OSB. It is made of strands or chips of wood that are glued together under great pressure. You can also buy grooved and primed OSB panels, which have vertical grooves typically spaced 8″ apart and are painted with a primer coat. These cost more but will give your clubhouse an instant finished look. Get the ⅜″-thick sheets, which are easiest to put up.

You can also get CDX plywood. Plywood is made up of plies, which are thin layers of wood laid crosswise over each other and then glued together under pressure. CDX plywood has a fairly smooth C-grade side, a rougher D-grade side (with knotholes or cracks), and an exterior glue so it won't fall apart in the rain. OSB and plywood normally come in 4-foot by 8-foot sheets, though some lumberyards sell 2-foot by 4-foot "handy panels." For a clubhouse, I'd recommend 4-foot by 8-foot panels that are ⅞₆″ or ½″ thick.

Flooring

Generally, any boards ¾″ thick will work fine for flooring. You can use decking boards, so called because they're used for backyard decks; they are usually 5½″ wide and a full 1″ thick. They can be expensive, though, and usually are pressure-treated, so you'd need to wear a dust mask while sawing these boards. In addition, some varieties of decking are now made of plastic, requiring a drill and special screws.

Some lumberyards sell ranch-grade boards, made of rough pine. These might be a good, cheap alternative for flooring if they are not too warped and don't have big knotholes.

If you are buying wood and you can use a power saw — or someone can help you with one — buy two sheets of ¾″-thick tongue-and-groove OSB for your floor. This stuff, sometimes called Sturd-I-Floor, is less expensive than boards and is very strong. It's what builders use for house floors. It comes in 4-foot by 8-foot sheets, which may be more than you need, but you can use the extra on a wall or the roof. Just remember, it's thicker than the ½″ OSB or plywood you might be using on the walls.

Roofing

A clubhouse roof has two parts: the boards that make it strong, and the roofing or roof covering that keeps the rain out.

For the boards, you can use ¾″-thick standard boards, car siding, or 1″-thick decking. Plywood or OSB will also work for your roof, but be sure to

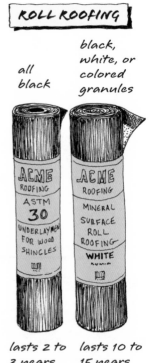

ROLL ROOFING

all black

black, white, or colored granules

lasts 2 to 3 years   *lasts 10 to 15 years*

use ⅝"- or ¾"-thick sheets because the roof beams are spaced too far apart for the thinner sheets. For its price, strength, and good looks, I recommend car siding.

Many roof coverings are available, and since you're building a small structure, you may be able to find enough leftovers from another building project. Ask your neighbors or local contractors. Lumberyards also might have odd piles of roof covering in their "bargain area." Acceptable roof coverings are roll roofing, asphalt or fiberglass roof shingles, metal sheets, or just about anything else that will shed water and not rot. (Note that if you use metal roofing, you'll need metal-working tools to cut it and fasten it in place.) If you have to buy roofing, look for either 30-pound felt, which is a felt fabric soaked in tar (also called tar paper), or mineral-coated roll roofing, which is a thicker felt tar paper covered with fine colored gravel and lasts much longer.

Nails and Screws

When you look for fasteners (nails, screws, and bolts) at a hardware store, you'll find rows and rows of them displayed in little boxes. The boxes of nails have labels describing the kinds of nails they hold and their size, such as 4d, 8d, 16d, etc. These sizes are based on the old English pennyweight system that refers to their length. For example, a 10d, or 10 penny nail, is 3" long. You'll be using mostly 6d to 16d nails. Here are the kinds of fasteners you'll most likely need:

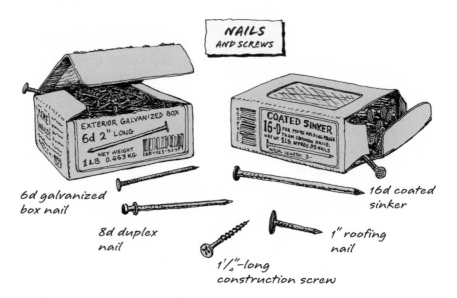

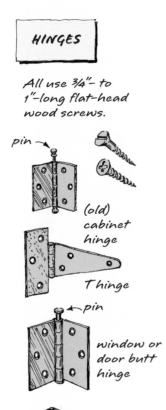

HINGES

All use ¾"- to 1"-long flat-head wood screws.

pin

(old) cabinet hinge

T hinge

← pin

window or door butt hinge

small utility hinge

- **Coated sinkers.** Coated sinkers are the cheapest nails to buy and the easiest to pound in. Sinkers are coated with a greenish plastic film that makes them easy to "sink" into the wood. The same coating also sticks to the wood once the nails are in, giving the nails great holding power. All the builders in the country use them. You will want 12d or 16d (your choice) coated sinkers to nail the 2×4s together, and 6d or 8d (your choice) coated sinkers to nail the sheathing to the 2×4s.

- **Duplex nails.** These nails are used for temporary bracing. They have two heads so that when you no longer need the bracing you can easily pull out the nails. For starters, buy a 1-pound box of 6d.

- **Galvanized box nails.** Because they're galvanized, these nails won't rust, and they're best for your clubhouse exterior trim boards. Get a 1-pound box of 6d.

- **Galvanized roofing nails.** For the roof, buy a 1-pound box of 1"-long galvanized roofing nails. These have extra-wide heads on them to hold down tar paper, roll roofing, or roof shingles.

- **Construction screws** (optional). These come in similar boxes as the nails and are commonly 1" to 5" long. Get a 1-pound box of 1¼"-long Phillips-head construction screws if you are going to build your own door. They also work well for screwing in hinges.

Hinges

You'll need hinges for your door. If you're reusing a door, use the original hinges that came with it. If it has no hinges, ordinary door hinges will work fine. If you have to buy new hinges, get a set of two T hinges, which are used for gates and shed doors. (See the door-hanging section on page 82 for more on doors and hinges.)

Okay, now you know enough about building materials to get you on your way. Make a materials list, and take it with you to the lumberyard. You might want to use the materials list for the Classic Clubhouse (see page 53) if your plan is similar. Don't hesitate to use the carpentry words we've discussed when asking for wood at the lumberyard. The sales staff will appreciate it.

A Note to Parents

Perhaps your offspring have asked you to build a clubhouse for them or you are thinking of building one for them. Ideally, your kids will want to build all or most of it themselves, but they may still need help finding the right tools and getting the lumber.

Will it be worth it? You bet!

Building something like this with your kids (or letting them build it) is a powerful trust-and-confidence experience. You'll show your kids that you care about them and you trust them not to do stupid things with sharp tools. They will learn hands-on skills and gain confidence in their own ability to create something substantial.

Kids love it when you listen to them, and if they are spending more time indoors than seems healthy to you, ask them what they would like if they had a place of their own to play in. Then write down what they say.

You can try these "what if" questions:

- If you had a clubhouse, what would it look like?
- What would it look like inside?
- What would it have outside?
- What would you do in your clubhouse?
- What would you need to do these things?
- And the ultimate: What kind of clubhouse would you have if you could have anything you wanted in a playhouse or clubhouse?

These questions and any more you can think of are meant to trigger your kids' imaginations. Write down their answers. If they look at you funny or seem busy with their phones, then ask them to look at this book and let you know later what they would like to do. Leave some scratch paper and pencils out so they can write down ideas or draw plans.

More likely, your enthusiasm will be contagious, and your kids will love the idea. In this case, ask them what help they might need. If you agree to help them, then by all means follow through. Trust goes both ways.

If your kids are young, say 8 to 10 years of age, offer to help design and build their project, but give them as much space as you can. If they are 11 or older or think they can do it all themselves, try not to impose your presence any more than they request you to. Be patient as they learn to use tools for the first time. Banged fingers and maybe a nasty scratch from a handsaw are part of learning about tools.

If you help them with their desires and plans, try to steer them to a reasonably sized clubhouse. Suggest secret spaces, hidden exits, or cozy alcoves; kids love small, low-ceilinged places to curl up in. On the other hand, kids grow up, so allow room for a taller addition later. Don't forget windows for light and ventilation. If you have never built anything yourself, no problem; you can all be kids learning this together. The next chapters will guide you as well as your children through the process of building a permanent outdoor shelter.

Let the kids "improve" their clubhouse as much as they want to. Give them room to experiment with wild paint-color combinations, odd-shaped additions, and gardens if they desire. It may look like an eyesore at times, but if you limit the rules to tidying the yard and putting away the tools when they are finished, they will stay engaged with their clubhouse possibly for years . . . and you will know where they are!

Part 2

BUILDING A CLASSIC CLUBHOUSE

Okay, so you have your tools, a place to build, and maybe enough wood and nails. Great! Now let's get started.

Learning how to work with your hands by reading instructions from a book can be frustrating. If these instructions seem too long and you start to feel confused, look at the drawings for a while, then go back to the words. If you are actually building, concentrate on only one small part at a time, and then take a break. While your brain is absorbing information, your body is getting used to pounding, sawing, and lifting. You're learning a new set of skills here. Be patient. Breathe.

Here I'll take you through the steps of building what I call the Classic Clubhouse. This 6-foot by 8-foot building contains the basic elements of clubhouse construction. Feel free to use this design for your clubhouse, but if you want to design and build a different kind of clubhouse, by all means do so. The following chapters are only meant to show you how a clubhouse basically goes together.

You may also find yourself feeling stuck because you have different kinds of wood or different windows than the instructions call for. When this happens, and it will, step back and look at how the pieces of *your* clubhouse go together. You *will* be able to fix the problem, usually by adding or moving boards or by building a different kind of clubhouse. You can also build your clubhouse taller, shorter, or wider, or you can put the windows and door in different places. Whatever your building challenge, you'll figure it out, and you'll feel mighty good because you did it on your own.

Materials for Building the Classic Clubhouse

The materials on the list at right will allow you to build a 6-foot by 8-foot clubhouse. Each of the chapters that follows includes its own part of this list, so you can get the materials for each step of the process as you get there. Of course, if you like, you can copy this page, take it with you to the lumberyard, and come back with all you need for the entire construction. But don't forget about the recycled wood, windows, and other materials you might find along the way.

In sections that offer choices, I recommend the first item listed.

FLOOR PLAN FOR THE CLASSIC CLUBHOUSE

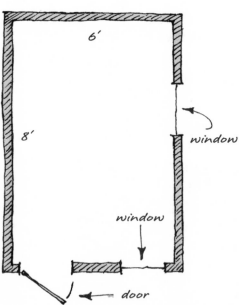

Classic Clubhouse Complete Materials List

Part	Quantity	Description
Foundation	4	pier blocks, concrete blocks, or large flat stones; *or*
	24	bricks
Foundation stakes	4	1×2 or 2×2 scraps, about 2 feet long
Foundation sills	2	4×4s, 8 feet long, pressure-treated
Floor joists	7	2×4s, 6 feet long
Floorboards	14	1×6 car siding or pine boards, 8 feet long; *or*
	1½	4 × 8-foot sheets ⅝"- or ¾"-thick plywood; *or*
	1½	4 × 8-foot sheets ¾"-thick tongue-and-groove OSB
Wall studs	20	2×4s, 6 feet long
Wall plates	4	2×4s, 8 feet long
	4	2×4s, 6 feet long
Upper roof beam	1	2×6, 8 feet long
Lower roof beam	1	2×4, 8 feet long
Bracing	8	1×4 furring strips or boards, 8 feet long
Wall sheathing	65	1×6 car siding or pine boards, 8 feet long; *or*
	5	4 × 8-foot sheets ⁷⁄₁₆"- or ½"-thick CDX plywood; *or*
	5	4 × 8-foot sheets ⁷⁄₁₆"- or ½"-thick OSB
Roof boards	20	1×6 car siding or pine boards, 8 feet long; *or*
	14	1×8 car siding or pine boards, 8 feet long
Roof covering	1	roll mineral-coated roofing (better) or 30-pound felt underlayment (okay)
Trim boards	2	1×3s or 1×4s, 10 feet long, for roof edging
Trim boards	14	1×3s or 1×4s, 8 feet long, for corners, doors, and windows
Windows	2	20" × 25" barn sash, or other size, depending on what you find
Window hinges	4	small utility or old cabinet hinges, with screws
Door	1	recycled or salvaged closet or other small door, or build one yourself (see page 81)
Door hinges	2	6"- or 8"-long T hinges, or 3" × 3" butt hinges, with screws
Nails	2 pounds of each	16d coated sinkers; 12d coated sinkers; 8d coated sinkers; 6d coated sinkers
Nails	1 pound of each	6d galvanized box nails, for the trim boards; 6d duplex nails, for the brace boards; ¾"- or 1"-long galvanized roofing nails
Screws	1 pound	1¼"-long Phillips-head construction screws (optional; useful if you're building your own door)

CHAPTER 3

BUILDING THE FOUNDATION AND FLOOR

It's time to dig in the dirt, set down a foundation, and build a floor. To start, you'll need your nine essential tools, plus a shovel and these materials listed below. Among the choices, I recommend the first item that is locally available or most affordable.

Foundation and Flooring Materials

Part	Quantity	Description
Foundation	4	pier blocks, concrete blocks, *or* large, flat stones; *or*
	24	bricks
Foundation stakes	4	1×2 or 2×2 scraps, about 2 feet long
Foundation sills	2	4×4s, 8 feet long, pressure-treated
Floor joists	7	2×4s, 6 feet long
Floorboards	14	1×6 car siding or pine boards, 8 feet long; *or*
	1½	4 × 8-foot sheets ⅝"- or ¾"-thick plywood; *or*
	1½	4 × 8-foot sheets ¾"-thick tongue-and-groove OSB (Sturd-I-Floor)
Nails	1 pound of each	6d coated sinkers; 8d coated sinkers; 6d or 8d galvanized box nails (optional; for nailing down floorboards)

Building the Foundation

The Classic Clubhouse is 6 feet wide and 8 feet long. To build its foundation, you'll need to set *cornerstones* of concrete blocks, bricks, or flat stones at each corner. If you have to buy your cornerstones, pier blocks or concrete blocks work best.

Look at your building site and decide where you want the corners of your clubhouse to be. If the site is cluttered with weeds or junk, clear it out before building. A clean site is a safe site. Start out by finding the foundation corners and pounding in stakes.

SET THE STAKES

Step 1. For your first corner, pound in a stake, which we'll call Stake #1.

Step 2. Hook your tape measure on the stake (or have your friend hold it there) and pull it to the 8-foot (96-inch) mark to find the location of Stake #2, and pound that one in.

Step 3. Now turn and measure 6 feet (72 inches) from Stake #2 to set Stake #3.

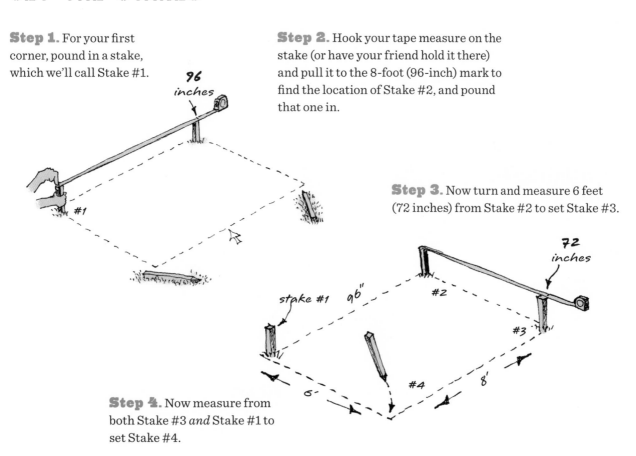

96 inches

72 inches

stake #1   96"   #2

#3

#1

#4

6'   8'

Step 4. Now measure from both Stake #3 *and* Stake #1 to set Stake #4.

SQUARE THE FOUNDATION

Once the stakes are in, check them to make sure your foundation is square. "Square" means that all four corners form a 90° angle.

Step 1. Get a friend to help you measure diagonally across your stakes (see the drawing at right). For a 6-foot by 8-foot foundation, the diagonal measurement will be exactly 10 feet.

Step 2. Pull up and reset the stakes until you get this measurement in both directions. This method works best on fairly flat ground, and don't worry if the diagonal measurements are off by up to an inch . . . you'll test this again when building the floor frame.

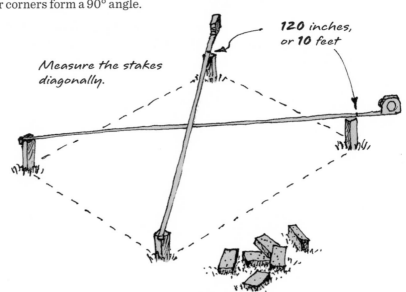

Measure the stakes diagonally.

120 inches, or 10 feet

SET AND LEVEL THE CORNERSTONES

The stakes now tell you exactly where the outer corners of your foundation stones are to be set.

Step 1. In each corner, dig out any loose dirt and grass for the cornerstone.

Step 2. When you're ready to set the cornerstone in place, take out the stake. Set the stone, adjusting it as necessary to make sure it's stable.

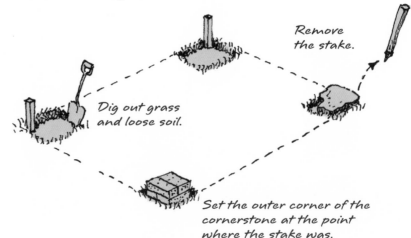

Remove the stake.

Dig out grass and loose soil.

Set the outer corner of the cornerstone at the point where the stake was.

Step 3. Level the cornerstones to ensure that the floor of the clubhouse will be level. You can check for level by laying a long, straight 2×4 across the top of each pair of cornerstones and setting your level on top of it, as shown in the drawing below. If the cornerstones aren't level, you may have to dig out more dirt from beneath one or more, or add bricks or stones. Then check for level again. Be patient; sometimes this takes a while, but starting with a level foundation is key to a successful clubhouse.

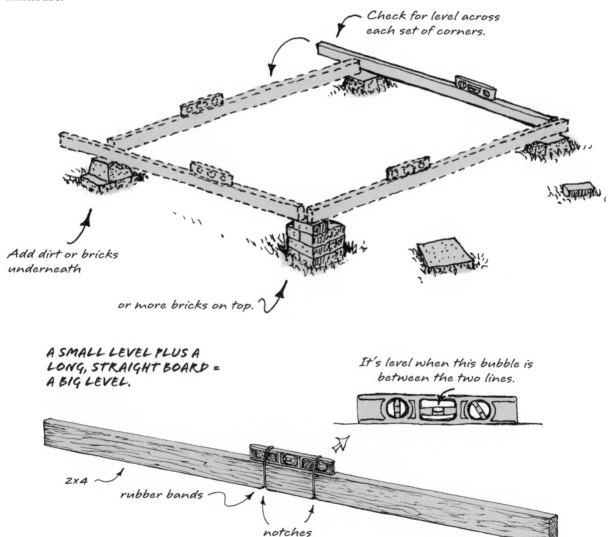

Check for level across each set of corners.

Add dirt or bricks underneath

or more bricks on top.

A SMALL LEVEL PLUS A LONG, STRAIGHT BOARD = A BIG LEVEL.

It's level when this bubble is between the two lines.

2×4

rubber bands

notches

The Floor Frame

Now you'll build a floor, beginning with 4×4 sills, which will support the 2×4 joists, which will support the floorboards. Yes, the 4×4s are big and heavy, but if you have a sharp handsaw, you'll be able to saw through them. Remember this: Before power saws and nail guns were invented, whole houses were once built with hand-saws and hammers.

CUT THE SILLS

Step 1. Set the 4×4 sills on your sawhorses, then get out your tape measure, pencil, and square. Measure to exactly 8 feet (96″) along the top of each 4×4, and mark that spot. If the sills are already 8 feet long, or within ¼″ of 8 feet, you lucked out. If not, use your square and draw a line across each 4×4 at that mark and also down the sides.

Step 2. Begin sawing the first sill. Your saw is nice and sharp, right? Take your time as you saw steadily through the 4×4. If it wiggles, have a helper hold it down. Use the line you drew as a guide, keeping the saw on the line. Make sure the piece you are cutting off is beyond the end of your sawhorses (not between them) so it will fall free.

Step 3. Do the same thing for the other sill. There! You just sawed through the thickest pieces of wood in your entire clubhouse.

MARK THE SILLS FOR THE JOISTS

Step 1. Lay both sills side by side on your sawhorses. Hook your tape measure to one end of one of the sills, and with your pencil, make a mark every 16″ to the other end.

Step 2. Using your square, draw lines over the marks across *both* sills. These will be the centerlines for your 2×4 floor joists (the boards that hold up the floorboards). This means that the joists will be centered over the lines. Tape measures usually have a little arrow at 16″, 32″, 48″, 64″, and every 16″ thereafter because this is the standard spacing of joists, studs, and rafters in house building.

Step 3. Once you've drawn all the centerlines, set the sills on the cornerstones. Set your level on each one to check for level, just to be certain.

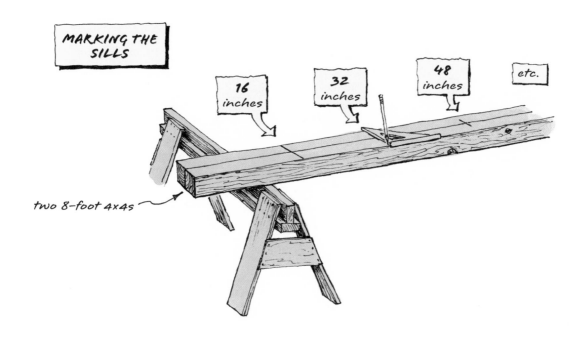

MARKING THE SILLS

16 inches

32 inches

48 inches

etc.

two 8-foot 4x4s

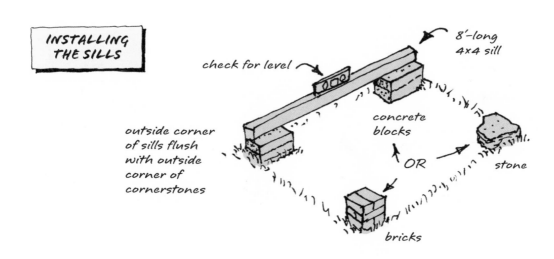

INSTALLING THE SILLS

check for level

8'-long 4x4 sill

outside corner of sills flush with outside corner of cornerstones

concrete blocks

OR

stone

bricks

INSTALL THE JOISTS

Step 1. For your floor joists, get seven 2×4s and place them on your sawhorses. Measure and mark each 2×4 at 6 feet long, then draw a cut line using your square. Saw them all to length (unless you lucked out again), sawing slowly and watching your cut lines. Then take a break; that was a lot of sawing.

Step 2. Set your joists on the sills so they are centered on the centerline marks, then put your level on them for one more test. You might have to add a shingle or thin piece of wood under one or more of the sill ends to finally get the whole thing level. Keep at it!

Step 3. Once the joists are level, nail them to the sills with 6d nails. You'll have to toenail them — that is, drive a nail at an angle through one and into the other. The best way is to hold the joist in place with your knee, tap the nail into the side or end of the joist, near the bottom, and then drive the nail at an angle until it "bites" into the sill. (See the drawing below.) This can be tricky at first, but toenailing will get easier after some practice.

Step 4. If your floor is crooked, meaning not square and level, it will be a lot harder to build the rest of your clubhouse, so test your floor frame for squareness again by measuring the diagonals. Hook your tape to one corner of your floor, pull it diagonally to the far corner, and see if you get 10 feet, or 120″. If it's longer, have a friend hold down or sit on the far corner of the floor frame while you push the opposite (diagonal corner) toward him or her to lessen the long measurement. Continue until the diagonals are both the same.

Step 5. Test the frame for level one more time because all the nailing and nudging might have moved things.

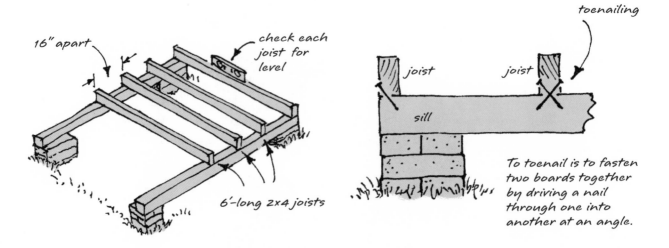

16″ apart

check each joist for level

6′-long 2x4 joists

toenailing

joist   joist

sill

To toenail is to fasten two boards together by driving a nail through one into another at an angle.

Once you've gotten this far, take a break. Go swimming, eat lunch, or do something else because you just did a *lot* of building!

Putting Down the Floorboards

Ready to continue? Let's put down the floorboards. Any boards, plywood, or OSB panels will work fine, even in combination, so long as all the boards are the same thickness. Car siding, nailed with the grooves facing down, makes a nice, tight floor.

HOW TO INSTALL FLOORBOARDS

Step 1. Set some floorboards on your sawhorses. Measure and cut the boards so they either go across all your joists (8 feet long) or will end over the center of a joist. Since your joists are all 16" apart, the floorboards will be 16", 32", 46", 64", 80", or 96" long. The longer the better, and every board must end over the middle of a joist.

Step 2. Nail the boards to every joist with 8d nails.

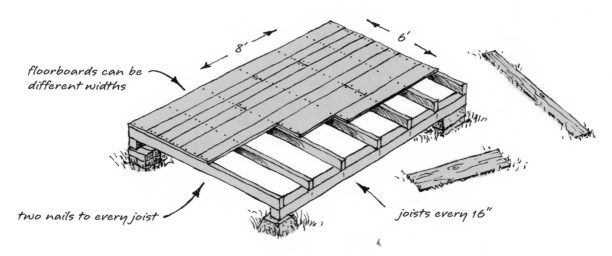

floorboards can be different widths

two nails to every joist

joists every 16"

Shorter boards should always meet over the middle of a joist.

HOW TO INSTALL PLYWOOD OR OSB PANELS

Step 1. If you're using sheets of plywood or OSB, first cut them to size, then set them over the joists. Remember to use ⅝"- or ¾"-thick plywood or OSB. If your floor frame is square, a 4-foot by 8-foot sheet should fit nicely on your joists, without any cutting.

Step 2. Start a nail in each corner of a sheet or panel to set it in place, then pound in a nail every 6" along the outside edges and every 12" on the inside joists. Use 8d nails.

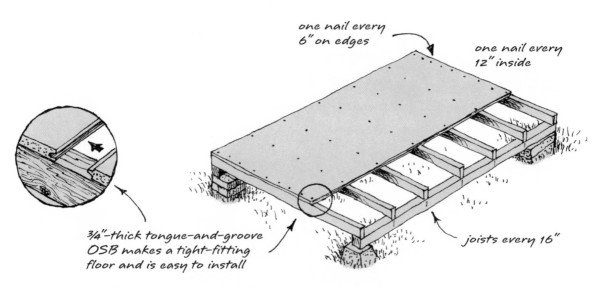

one nail every 6" on edges

one nail every 12" inside

¾"-thick tongue-and-groove OSB makes a tight-fitting floor and is easy to install

joists every 16"

Okay, now you have a floor that will last for years. Time for a snack!

CHAPTER 4

FRAMING THE WALLS AND ROOF

With the foundation and floor complete, you can build the frame, or skeleton, of your clubhouse. All of the wall frames will have top and bottom 2×4 pieces, called plates, and vertical 2×4 pieces, called studs. Assemble the wall frames on the ground, then set up each frame one by one on the floor. Three of the walls will be 66" high and the fourth one 9" taller, or 75" high, so the roof can slope. The roof frame will consist of only two beams, a 2×4 and a 2×6, both 8 feet long.

Materials List for Walls and Roof Frame

To build your walls and roof frame, you'll need your nine essential tools, a stepladder, and the materials listed on the following page. You'll also need a large, flat spot near your floor on which to put the wall frames together.

Framing Materials

Part	Quantity	Description
Wall plates	4	2×4s, 8 feet long
	4	2×4s, 6 feet long
Wall studs	20	2×4s, 6 feet long
Upper roof beam	1	2×6, 8 feet long
Lower roof beam	1	2×4, 8 feet long
Bracing	8	1×4 furring strips or boards, 8 feet long
Nails	2 pounds of each	16d coated sinkers; 12d coated sinkers; 8d coated sinkers; 6d coated sinkers
Nails	1 pound	6d duplex nails, for the brace boards

Building Wall 1

Let's build the tall wall first. This wall will be 8 feet long, the same length as the floor, and won't have any doors or windows.

FRAME WALL 1

Step 1. First you'll make the plates. Set two 2×4s that are at least 8 feet long on your sawhorses. Measure the 2×4s, and if they're not 8 feet long (or within ¼″ of it), cut them to length.

Step 2. Put the plates together, on edge, on your sawhorses. Hook your measuring tape to one end, and make marks at 24″, 48″, and 72″. With your pencil and square, draw a centerline across both boards at each mark. The centerline will show where the center of each stud will go. Set the plates aside.

Step 3. For the studs, set out five 2×4s that are 6 feet or longer on your sawhorses. Since wall 1 will be 75″ high and the thicknesses of the two plates together add up to 3″, then the studs will be 72″ long (75″ − 3″ = 72″), or 6 feet. Measure the 2×4s, and if they're not 6 feet (or within ¼″ of it), cut them to length.

Step 4. Lay the plates and studs on edge on the ground so that the centers of your studs meet the centerlines on the plates (see the drawing on facing page). Using 12d or 16d nails, drive two nails through the plates into the ends of each stud, as shown. As you hammer, hold down each stud with your knee, or step on it, so it will stay put. Your tall wall is now framed.

INSTALL WALL 1

Step 1. With a friend's help, carry the wall frame to the floor and set it in place.

Step 2. Nail the wall down by driving one or two 12d nails between each stud through the bottom plate and into the floor. While your friend holds the frame, use your level to check whether the wall is plumb (straight up and down). If it isn't, ask your friend to nudge the wall frame until the bubble in your level is in the middle.

Step 3. To keep the wall plumb, nail on temporary brace boards, as shown on the drawing below. Here it can be helpful to have three people working: one to hold and adjust the wall, one to check for level, and one to attach the bracing. You will pry off the brace boards later, so don't nail them in too tight. Use 6d duplex nails, the two-headed nails that are easy to pull out.

The Right Nails

Always use 12d or 16d nails when nailing through 2×4s. Although 6d or 8d nails work well for toenailing 2×4s, such as when attaching the joists to the 4×4 sills, they are not strong enough to hold 2×4s together. The 6d or 8d nails also work fine for nailing in brace boards, floorboards, and sheathing.

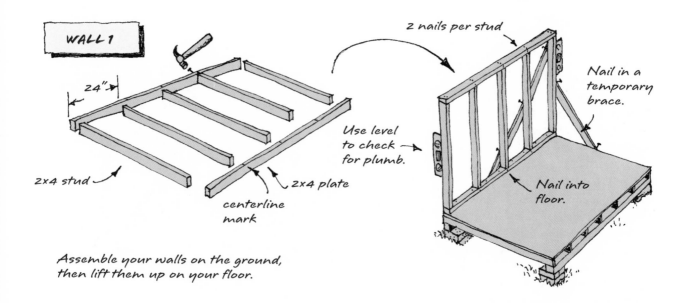

WALL 1

24"

2×4 stud

centerline mark

2×4 plate

Use level to check for plumb.

2 nails per stud

Nail in a temporary brace.

Nail into floor.

Assemble your walls on the ground, then lift them up on your floor.

Building Wall 2

The second wall, which will be 66" tall, will be shorter than the 6-foot width of the floor because it will be set between the two longer walls. These wall frames are each 3½" thick (the width of a 2×4), so they add up to a total thickness of 7". Wall 2, then, will be 72" – 7", or 65" wide.

FRAME WALL 2

Step 1. Set out two 2×4s that are at least 6 feet long on your sawhorses. These will be the top and bottom plates. Measure and cut them to 65" long.

Step 2. Put the plates together, on edge, on your sawhorses. With your square and tape measure, measure from one end (it doesn't matter which end), and draw centerline marks at 24" and 48" on both plates. Set them aside.

Step 3. Set out four more 6-foot-long 2×4s on your sawhorses. These will be the studs. Measure and cut them to 63" long. (If this wall is 66" high, and the top and bottom plates together are 3" thick, then the studs will be 66" – 3", or 63" long.)

Step 4. Lay the four studs on the ground with the plates so the center of each stud meets a centerline on the plates (see the drawing below). Nail the plates to the studs as you did with the tall wall. Wall 2 is now framed.

INSTALL WALL 2

Step 1. Get a friend to help lift up and brace this wall next to the tall wall.

Step 2. Nail the bottom plate into the floor and the end stud into the end stud of wall 1. Use a level to get the wall plumb, having your friend nudge the wall as needed.

Step 3. Nail in another brace to hold it in place (see the drawing at right).

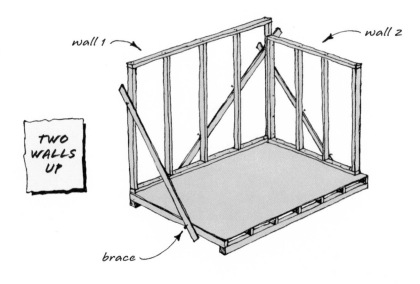

wall 1

wall 2

TWO WALLS UP

brace

Building Wall 3 (with a Door and Window)

The third wall will be the same size as wall 2, and it will have the door and a window. You'll need to know the sizes of these openings before building the wall. In this example, you will build openings to fit a door 24″ wide and 60″ tall and a window that is 20″ wide and 25″ tall. If you have different door and window sizes, simply substitute the correct measurements.

CUT AND MARK THE PLATES

Step 1. On your sawhorses, cut two 2×4s to 65″ long, as you did for wall 2. These will be the top and bottom plates.

Step 2. Set the plates together, on edge, on your sawhorses. From the left end, measure to 25¾″, draw a line across both plates, and draw an X to the *right* of the line on both plates.

Step 3. From the right end, measure to 21¾″, draw a line across both plates, and draw an X to the *left* of that line on both plates.

Step 4. Draw an X at each end of the plates. The Xs are where the studs go.

Step 5. Write a "T" for "top plate" on the upper 2×4, and a "B" for "bottom plate" on the lower 2×4 (see the drawing below). Once the boards are marked, there should be a 24¼″-wide space for the door at the left, and a 20¼″-wide space for the window at the right, as shown in the drawing below.

Step 6. Set the plates aside.

Centerlines, Edge Lines, and Xs

House builders use their own language to mark the position of studs and other pieces of wood in wall framing. The simplest mark is the centerline — a line to mark the center of the stud where it meets the plate, which we used in walls 1 and 2. Another mark is an edge line with an X. For wall 3, we are using edge lines and Xs to tell us more accurately where the pieces go to fit the door and the window.

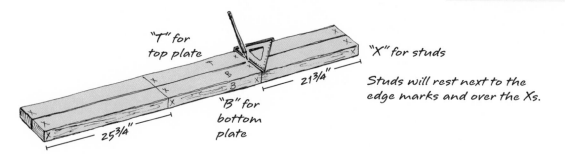

"T" for top plate
"B" for bottom plate
"X" for studs
21¾″
25¾″

Studs will rest next to the edge marks and over the Xs.

INSTALL THE STUDS

Step 1. On your sawhorses, cut four 2×4 studs 63″ long, as you did for wall 2.

Step 2. Lay out the studs on the ground with the two wall plates, so the studs all meet the plates at the Xs. Nail the plates to the studs, stepping or kneeling on each stud to hold it in place.

Step 3. For the blocks that frame the door and window openings, measure 6″ down all four studs from the top of the wall plate, then draw an edge line and an X *above* the edge line. These four Xs show where the door and window header blocks will go.

Step 4. Along the two right-hand studs, measure another 25¼″ from the first line you drew, then draw another edge line and an X *below* that line. These two Xs show where the window rough-sill block will go (see drawing on facing page).

INSTALL THE BLOCKING

Step 1. Cut two 2×4s to 20¼″ long. These will frame the top and bottom of your window.

Step 2. Set the blocks in place beside the studs at the Xs you just drew. You should end up with a window opening that is 25¼″ high by 20¼″ wide.

Step 3. If your window is 25″ by 20″, drop it in gently to see if it will fit. It does? Good! Now take it out. If it doesn't fit, push on a corner of the wall frame to make it more square, then try again. If it still doesn't fit, you may have to adjust the blocks or move a stud.

Step 4. Cut one more 2×4 to 24¼″ long. This will frame the top of your doorway. If you have a door already, see if it will fit. Otherwise, you can build a door to fit later.

Step 5. Nail these blocks to the studs by using two 12d or 16d nails through each stud into the blocks.

INSTALL WALL 3

Step 1. With a friend's help, set this wall in place and brace it as you did the others.

Step 2. Nail it down, first into the floor and then into the adjoining wall corners. Do *not* nail it to the floor in the doorway, where you'll cut off the bottom plate. (In

fact, once wall 3 is up, you can use your handsaw to cut off this bottom plate that spans the doorway at any time.)

Step 3. Plumb the wall with your level while your friend helps nudge the frame, then brace it in place.

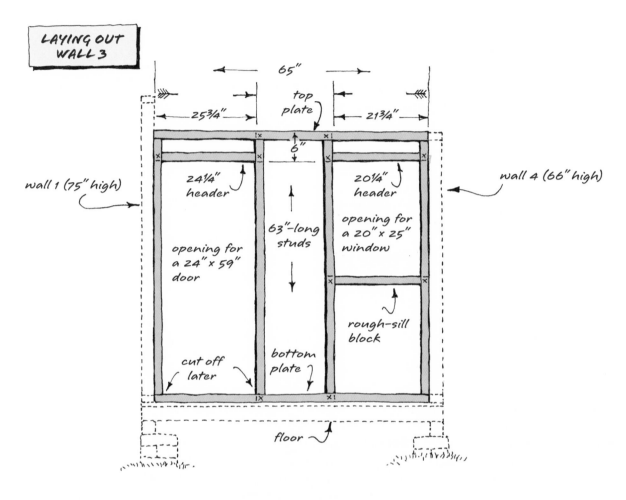

LAYING OUT WALL 3

65"

25¾"

top plate

21¾"

6"

wall 1 (75" high)

24¼" header

wall 4 (66" high)

20¼" header

opening for a 24" x 59" door

63"-long studs

opening for a 20" x 25" window

rough-sill block

cut off later

bottom plate

floor

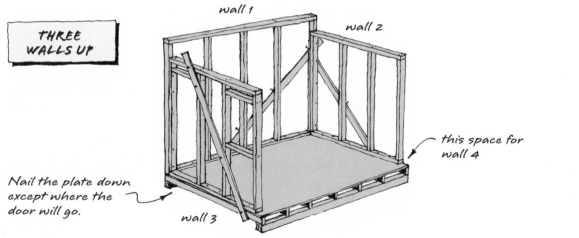

THREE WALLS UP

wall 1

wall 2

this space for wall 4

Nail the plate down except where the door will go.

wall 3

Building Wall 4

Wall 4 is also 66″ tall and 8 feet (96″) long. This wall will have one window, which I will show you how to frame in three different sizes.

FRAME WALL 4

Step 1. Lay out two 2×4s on your sawhorses for your plates, and cut them to 96″ long.

Step 2. Set them on edge side by side, then measure out and mark every 24″, as before. Draw the centerlines on both plates, then set the plates aside.

Step 3. Lay out five more 2×4s for studs, then measure and cut these to 63″ long.

Step 4. Nail the plates and studs of this wall together as you did the others, and leave it on the ground. It's getting a little easier, right?

FRAME THE WINDOW

On this wall, you will frame the window in a slightly different way than in wall 3.

Step 1. Choose the two studs that will surround your window. On each of these two studs, measure and draw an edge line 6″ down from the top of the wall, then draw an X above the line.

Step 2. Measure another 25¼″ from the first edge line, draw another edge line, then an X below that line. These two Xs show where the window rough-sill block will go (see the drawing on facing page).

Step 3. Measure the space between the two studs, which should be about 22½″. Cut two 2×4 blocks that long, set them on the Xs, and nail them into the frame. These blocks are your window header and rough sill.

Step 4. Measure to 20¼″ on both the header and rough sill, draw an edge line, then an X beyond the edge line.

Step 5. Measure and cut another 2×4 block, called a trimmer, to 25¼″ long.

Step 6. Nail the trimmer block in place on the Xs (see the drawing on facing page).

Window Safety

For safety, use only windows in wood or metal frames, instead of sheets of glass. Also, the bottom of any window should be far enough above the floor, at least 12″, so that someone doesn't kick it or crash into it during rough play.

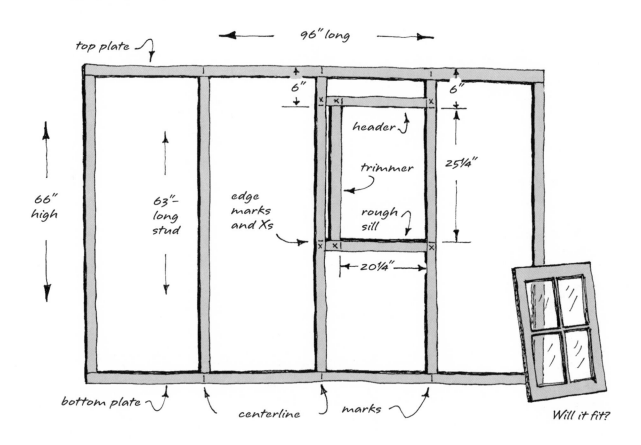

LAYING OUT
WALL 4

top plate

96" long

6"

6"

header

trimmer

25¼"

rough
sill

66"
high

63"-
long
stud

edge
marks
and Xs

20¼"

bottom plate

centerline

marks

Will it fit?

Bonus: How to Frame Bigger Windows

If you have to cut through a stud to accommodate a big window, frame the wall as shown here, with a full stud to each side of the window opening. The short stud pieces above the window header and below the window rough sill are called cripples.

If you have to cut through two studs to accommodate an even bigger window, frame the wall as illustrated below. The header should be a 4×4 or two 2×4s nailed together, and it should be long enough to span the window opening plus the thickness of the two trimmer pieces that hold it up.

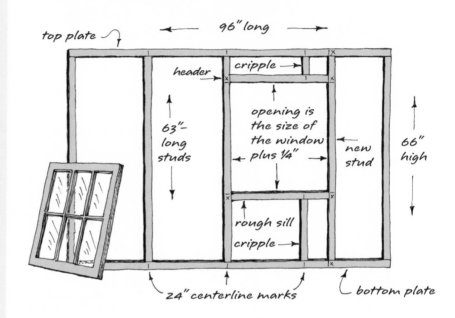

WALL 4 WITH A BIG WINDOW

top plate

96" long

header

cripple

63"-long studs

opening is the size of the window plus ¼"

new stud

66" high

rough sill

cripple

24" centerline marks

bottom plate

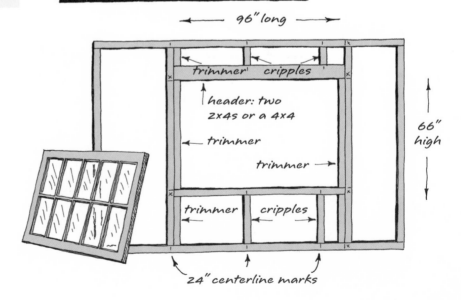

WALL 4 WITH A BIGGER WINDOW

96" long

trimmer   cripples

header: two 2x4s or a 4x4

trimmer

trimmer

66" high

trimmer   cripples

24" centerline marks

INSTALL WALL 4

Step 1. With your friend's help, set this wall in place and brace it as you did the others.

Step 2. Nail it down, first into the floor and then into the adjoining wall corners.

Step 3. Plumb it with your level while your friend helps nudge the frame, then nail in another brace board.

FOUR
WALLS UP

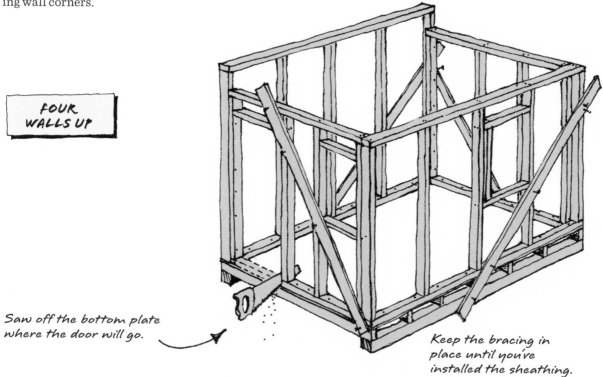

Saw off the bottom plate where the door will go.

Keep the bracing in place until you've installed the sheathing.

You did it! All the walls are framed, and it's time for another break.

Framing the Roof

Now we'll need to put up two beams, a 2×6 and a 2×4, both 8 feet long, to hold up the roof boards.

CUT AND INSTALL THE ROOF BEAMS

Step 1. Find a stepladder and climb up to look at the top of one of your 6-foot-wide short walls. Hook your measuring tape to the outer edge of the tall wall, measure to 24″ along the top of the 6-foot wall, and draw a centerline. Then pull the tape farther along and draw another centerline at 42″.

Step 2. Go around to the other short wall and draw similar centerlines the same distances from the tall-wall edge. These will mark the *approximate* places for the beams.

Step 3. Set the 2×6 and 2×4 on your sawhorses. Measure them; if they're not 8 feet long, cut them to length. These will be your roof beams.

Step 4. With a friend's help, haul the roof beams up to the roof and stand them on edge on top of your short walls, aligned over the Xs. The 2×6 will be the upper roof beam, positioned closer to

wall 1. The 2×4 will be the lower roof beam, positioned closer to wall 3. Don't nail them in yet.

Step 5. Lay a straight board, or your long level, across the beams and the wall tops. Adjust your two beams by nudging them until the board rests on both of them. If you move the beams off the centerlines you drew, that's okay.

Step 6. When you have the beams positioned so that the board just touches the wall 1 top plate, the two roof beams, and the wall 3 top plate, toenail the beams into the top plates of walls 2 and 4, as shown.

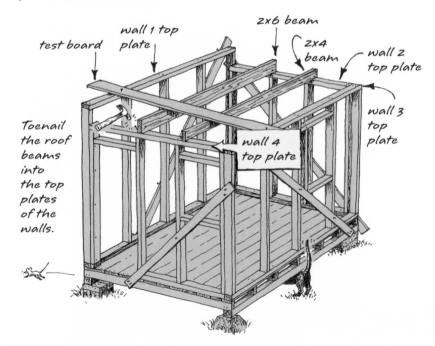

Toenail the roof beams into the top plates of the walls.

test board

wall 1 top plate

2×6 beam

2×4 beam

wall 2 top plate

wall 3 top plate

wall 4 top plate

NINETEENTH-CENTURY VICTORIAN PLAYHOUSE

The Park-McCullough House is one of the finest and best-preserved Victorian houses in New England. The 35-room mansion is situated on a 200-acre estate in North Bennington, Vermont. Built in 1865, the house is on the National Register of Historic Places. The grounds are open to the public daily, the house by appointment only.

❝ This playhouse is behind the Park-McCullough House in North Bennington, Vermont. The playhouse was originally built as a doghouse in 1865 and later converted for the children. It is fully furnished, complete with period wallpaper, and features a child-size cast-iron cookstove."

— *Melissa Segalla, curator of the Park-McCullough House*

CHAPTER 5

FINISHING

Now it's time to enclose your clubhouse with sheathing, which can be boards, plywood, or OSB panels. Then you'll put on the door, windows, and trim boards. Again, you'll need your essential tools, along with a utility knife, a stepladder, and the materials listed on the facing page.

Sheathing and Siding in One

Car siding and board-and-batten are two materials that can serve as both sheathing and finish siding. If you have to buy new sheathing, these might be the best options, since they aren't very expensive and can double as your finished outside siding. Car siding works equally well for the floor and the roof.

Grooved and primed OSB can also serve as both sheathing and finish siding. If you want to use it for finish siding, carefully measure it so the edges of the panels are centered over studs and the grooves are always outside and vertical for a good look.

See chapter 7 for more on finish siding and how to install it.

Finishing Materials

Part	Quantity	Description
Walls	65	1×6 car siding or pine boards, 8 feet long; *or*
	5	4 × 8-foot sheets ⁷⁄₁₆"- or ½"-thick CDX plywood; *or*
	5	4 × 8-foot sheets ⁷⁄₁₆"- or ½"-thick OSB
Roof boards	20	1×6 car siding or pine boards, 8 feet long; *or*
	14	1×8 car siding or pine boards, 8 feet long
Roof covering	1	roll mineral-coated roofing (better) or 30-pound felt underlayment (okay)
Trim boards	2	1×3s or 1×4s, 10 feet long, for roof edging
Trim boards	14	1×3s or 1×4s, 8 feet long, for corners, doors, and windows
Windows	2	20" × 25" barn sash, or other size, depending on what you find
Window hinges	2–4	small utility or old cabinet hinges, with screws
Door	1	recycled or salvaged closet or other small door, or one that you build yourself (see how to build a door on page 81)
Door hinges	2	6"- or 8"-long T hinges, or 3" × 3" butt hinges, with screws
Nails	2 pounds of each	8d coated sinkers; 6d coated sinkers
Nails	1 pound of each	6d galvanized box nails, for the trim boards; 6d duplex nails, for the brace boards; ¾"- or 1"-long galvanized roofing nails
Screws	1 pound	1¼"-long Phillips-head construction screws (optional; useful if you're building your own door)

Covering the Walls

The sheathing is the exterior covering of the clubhouse, and it also strengthens and braces the framing. So take off the brace boards only when you are about to cover the wall they are bracing. Here are some tips:

- Nail on sheathing boards across the studs starting at the bottom of each wall. By "bottom," I mean that the sheathing should cover the 2×4 joists but not the 4×4 sill.

- Always join boards or panels over a stud so the ends or edges are nailed to something solid (see the drawing on page 117).

- Use 8d nails for boards, driving in two or three nails at the ends of each board and two nails on every inside stud. Use 6d nails for thin plywood or OSB sheathing, nailing them every 6″ on the edges and every 12″ on the inside studs.

- Install sheathing right up to the edges of window and door openings, notching or ripping it as necessary so it sits flush with the edges of the openings.

- When you get to the top of a wall, mark the last board with a pencil line, saw off the extra wood, then nail up the board.

- To mark the top of a board on the slanted wall, put a roof board against it, and mark the wall board edge minus the thickness of the roof board (see the drawing below).

SHEATHING A
WALL WITH A
SLANTED TOP

Mark and cut the sheathing so it fits under the edge of the roof board.

Roofing with Car Siding

If you are using car siding, mark the boards for the overhang as described on the facing page. Trim the tongue off the outer edge of one board with your handsaw, then nail the board on at the edge of the roof as described. Working your way across the roof, nail on the remaining boards with the grooved side facing down, joining them one at a time. As you approach the other edge of the roof, cut or rip the last board lengthwise to make it fit, and then nail it down. Add the trim boards as described. (For more on installing car siding, see page 116.)

Building the Roof

A flat roof will leak, even with tar paper on it, so your roof should be slanted and extend beyond the walls to help keep them dry. For the roof boards, I recommend using pine boards or 1×6 or 1×8 car siding. The boards should be about 7'6" (90") long to allow for an overhang at both ends. For added strength around the edges of your roof, add 1×3 or 1×4 trim boards.

INSTALL THE ROOF BOARDS AND TRIM

Step 1. Set your roof boards on your sawhorses, and cut them all to 7'6" long.

Step 2. On each roof board, measure and mark a line 8 inches in from one end, to mark the spot where the overhang will start.

Step 3. Place one of the boards across the roof, on one of the outside edges, slanting down from the tall wall to the opposite wall. Align the overhang mark at the outside edge of the short or tall wall. Align the long edge of the board so that it covers the top edge of the sheathing on the side wall. (If there is no sheathing yet, tack on a ¾"-thick piece of scrap to the wall framing to use as a guide.)

Step 4. Nail the roof board into the top wall plates and the roof beams with 8d nails.

Step 5. Repeat the process with another roof board at the other side of the roof.

Step 6. Nail on all the remaining roof boards, being sure to align the overhang marks. When it comes to installing the last board, you may find yourself with a gap that the board doesn't quite fit into. In this case you'll have to rip the board (cut it the long way) or find a narrow board to fit.

Step 7. Using 6d galvanized box nails, nail on trim boards all around the edges of the roof. Use the 10-foot-long 1×3 or 1×4 furring strips on the long edges of the roof, and the 8-foot-long furring strips on the shorter walls, cutting them to size as necessary. (If you haven't yet installed the wall sheathing, though, hold off on installing the trim on the short walls until after you've nailed on the sheathing.)

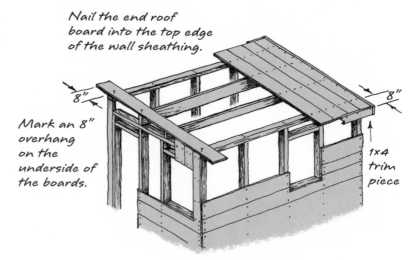

Nail the end roof board into the top edge of the wall sheathing.

Mark an 8" overhang on the underside of the boards.

8"

8"

1×4 trim piece

COVER WITH ROLL ROOFING

Cover your roof with 30-pound felt (tar paper) or, for a more permanent roof, mineral-coated roll roofing. One roll should be enough. (You can also use 15-pound felt with asphalt shingles, which I talk about in chapter 11.)

Step 1. On the ground, roll out a length of roll roofing and measure a piece that will be 2″ longer than the length of your roof. Measure the roof to double-check.

Step 2. Cut off the piece with a utility knife, using your square to set a board to cut against so you get a straight edge. Cut on the back side if you are cutting mineral-coated roofing.

Step 3. Roll up the piece, and carry it up to your roof. With a friend holding your ladder, set the piece of roofing along the lower edge, overhanging the trim board by 1″. This allows for a "drip edge."

Step 4. Nail the roofing down with ¾″- or 1″-long roofing nails. Use one nail every 4″ along the bottom and side edges, and one nail every 12″ or so along the top edge.

Step 5. Cut and nail in a second piece of roofing, overlapping the first piece by at least 4″.

Step 6. Repeat with a third piece, allowing 1″ to hang over the top edge.

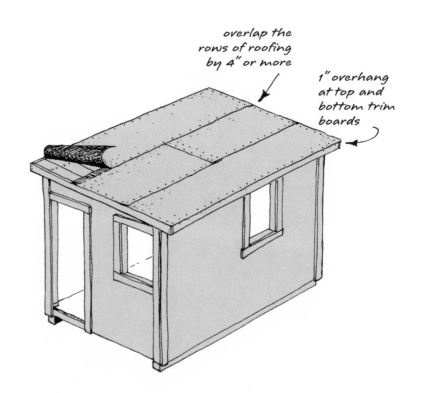

overlap the rows of roofing by 4″ or more

1″ overhang at top and bottom trim boards

Putting in the Door

Maybe you found a cool door at a recycled building-supply store or in an alley. An old-fashioned tall cabinet door might work or even a piece of plywood. Lumberyards often sell plywood in small sizes, typically called "handy panels." Ask for a 2-foot by 4-foot panel that is ¾" thick, which will make a good small door. If you can't find a door that fits, you can build your own door.

Whether you build your own or find a door, you'll need two hinges. Old door hinges or gate hinges will work fine. If you buy hinges, look for 6"-long T hinges, which are shaped like a T and meant for gates and shed doors (see the drawing on page 48). You'll also need ¾"- to 1¼"-long screws to hold them tight (nails will loosen up after a while).

BUILD YOUR OWN DOOR (OPTIONAL)

You can build your own door using 1×6 boards or car siding. Here's how.

Step 1. Measure your door opening, then subtract ¼" from the width (side to side) and 1" from the length (top to bottom); this is the size of the door you need.

Step 2. Lay out a few boards on your sawhorses, and measure the exact width you'll need. If you're lucky, you'll find the right width of boards to make up the door. Otherwise, first cut the boards to length, and then mark one of the boards to be cut lengthwise, or ripped, to make up the width you need. Use a straight board to draw this long cut line.

Step 3. Along the cut line, saw off, or rip, the extra part of the board. Be patient and get some help if you need it; it might take a while.

Step 4. Cut two crosspieces from 1×6 boards the width of the door.

Step 5. Assemble all the pieces on your sawhorses or on the ground, with the crosspieces over the top and bottom of the door.

Step 6. Square the door by measuring its diagonals as you did for the floor (see page 56).

continued on next page

¼" less than opening

1" shorter than opening

This brace keeps the door from sagging.

inside of door

Step 7. For the brace, lay another board diagonally over the crosspieces, from one edge of the door to the other.

Step 8. Mark cut lines at the points where the brace board crosses the crosspieces, then saw it to size (see the drawing on page 81).

Step 9. Nail or screw all the pieces together, being careful to keep the door square. This is where the 1¼″ construction screws can be used, for which you'll need a drill. Otherwise, drive 6d galvanized box nails through the door and bend them over.

Note: You can also make a door from plywood. Cut it to the size specified in step 1. If it is less than ¾″ thick, add crosspieces as described above to hold the hinge screws.

HANG THE DOOR

Step 1. Lay the door flat, then set the top hinge 4″ to 6″ down from the top of the door and the bottom hinge 6″ up from the bottom of the door. Use a pencil to mark the screw holes for each hinge.

Step 2. If you have a drill, use it to drill a *pilot hole* (a guide hole for a screw) at each mark, using a bit just a little narrower than the screws. If you don't have a drill, use a nail (again, just a little narrower than the screws), pounding it partway into each screw-hole mark and then pulling it out.

Step 3. Holding the hinges in place, screw in the screws. Be patient and keep at it.

Step 4. With help from a friend, set the door in place and wedge it with some shingles or shims, especially under the door, so it won't

stick when you close it. A door should have ⅛″ to ¼″ wiggle room on the top and sides and a ½″ to ¾″ gap on the bottom.

Step 5. Mark the location of the hinge screw holes on the adjacent wall, then make pilot holes, as you did on the door.

Step 6. Screw the hinges into the wall, and you have a door.

Hold with shingles or "shims."

Use a ¾″-thick block of wood as the bottom shim.

INSTALL THE KNOB, LATCH, AND DOORSTOP

Step 1. Once the door is hung on its hinges, put a handle or a knob on the outside of the door so you can open it, and another handle on the inside so you can pull it closed.

Step 2. So you can keep the door closed, put a latch on the outside of the door. The easiest way is to nail or screw on a piece of wood that you twist to hold the door shut. You can also add a hook-and-eye latch to close it from the inside.

Step 3. Have a friend (someone you trust) latch the door on the outside while you are inside. While the door is latched, nail on a piece of trim board, called a doorstop, onto the door frame, right up against the inside of the door. This will keep the door from opening too far inward and ripping off the hinges.

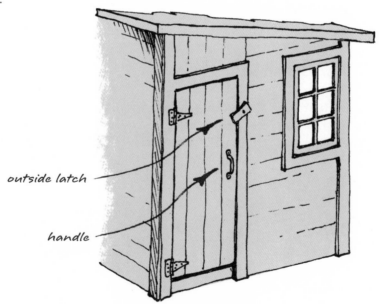

outside latch

handle

Putting on the Trim Boards and Windows

The trim boards not only make your clubhouse look good but may also help hold in your windows. A "fixed" window is one that doesn't open, so it doesn't require hinges. A hinged, openable window is nice for ventilation.

TRIM THE CORNERS

Step 1. At each corner of the clubhouse, measure from the bottom of the sheathing to the bottom edge of the roof to find the length of trim you'll need. Cut trim boards to length from 1×3 or 1×4 boards. On the slanted walls, cut one end of the trim board at a slight angle to fit snugly against the roof trim.

Step 2. Nail on all the trim boards with 6d galvanized box nails.

INSTALL A FIXED WINDOW

Step 1. Measure and cut the trim boards so that they will overlap the window opening by ½" on every side. Nail in place with 6d galvanized box nails.

Step 2. Set the window in the frame from the inside. Nail more trim boards on the inside to hold the window in.

Note: Be careful to fasten the inside trim boards only into the clubhouse framing and not into or through the window frame itself.

PUTTING
IN A FIXED
WINDOW

Sheathing is flush with the opening.

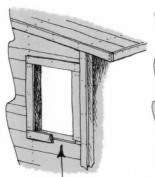

Trim boards overlap the outside edges of the window opening by ½".

Inside trim boards hold the window in place.

INSTALL AN INWARD-OPENING WINDOW

You can install an inward-opening window directly to the wall frame stud, or to the inside trim as shown below.

Step 1. Screw the hinges to the window frame.

Step 2. Set the window in its opening using thin wooden shims, as you did for the door (see page 82).

Step 3. Mark the screw holes for the hinges on the framing and then take the window out.

Step 4. Carefully make the pilot holes for the screws in the framing, then screw the hinges into it.

Step 5. Add a small trim board to the inside of the window opening to keep the hinges from ripping off.

Step 6. Add a cabinet knob or handle to open the window, and a latch to lock it.

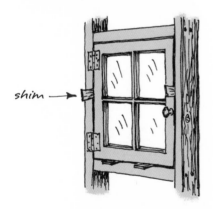

IF THE WINDOW WILL OPEN INWARD...

shim →

Hinge to the edge of the stud . . .

to the side of the stud . . .

window stops

or to the inside trim.

INSTALL AN OUTWARD-OPENING WINDOW

Step 1. Install the trim boards so they are flush with, rather than overlapping, the window frame. For now, leave off the trim board on the edge where the hinges will go.

Step 2. Set the window in place using some shims so it is even with the edges of the trim boards.

Step 3. Position the hinges where you want them. You can put hinges on the side of the window, but it is better to hinge an outside-opening window at the top so the wind doesn't blow it closed. Mark the screw holes with a pencil, then take out the window.

Step 4. Make all the pilot holes, then screw the hinges into the window frame.

Step 5. Put the window back in, and screw the hinges into the sheathing, as shown.

Step 6. Nail on the remaining trim board over the hinges.

Step 7. Put a narrow trim board on the inside of the window opening (like the doorstop) to stop the window from opening too far in and ripping off the hinges.

Step 8. Add a prop stick to hold the window open and a hook-and-eye latch on the inside if you want to lock the window shut.

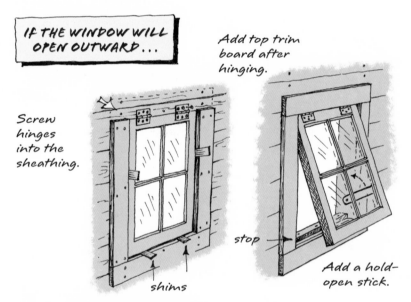

IF THE WINDOW WILL OPEN OUTWARD...

Screw hinges into the sheathing.

shims

Add top trim board after hinging.

stop

Add a hold-open stick.

Congratulations! You have a clubhouse! (Just don't forget to clean up the yard and put away those tools.)

Kids ▷ Reality Check

Have you been yelled at yet for messing up the yard? No? Good! But know this: Keep the yard or ground around your clubhouse clean even if no one has said anything. This way, you'll not only get to keep your clubhouse, but you'll also be more likely to get permission to continue improving it. This is good for safety, too. If the treasures you and your friends have brought in for your clubhouse are scattered all over the yard, your parents might immediately think, "junk," so keep these items out of sight as much as possible. Also, if these same parents have to pick up the tools you've been using, you might not see those tools again. So when you have finished building for the day, put away all your tools, and pile everything from your project out of the way as neatly as possible.

When your clubhouse is finished, take an extra hour or so to store away the usable scraps and other treasures, and then go over the entire site to pick up all those little scraps, nails, and other junk hiding in the grass. You won't want these getting under the lawn mower. Finally, put the tools back where you (or their owner) can easily find them. This exercise in thoughtfulness will help you in many ways, guaranteed!

KATE'S VICTORIAN HOUSE

Jack and Lin Presbury, of Staunton, Virginia, built this delightful playhouse for their long-awaited daughter, Kate.

❝ My wife, Lin, and I had been married for 17 years when our child, Kate, was born. We have probably overdone it when it comes to giving her what she wants. For Kate's third birthday, I built a playhouse in the backyard. We wanted it to be special, as we live in a historic district where the neighbors would complain if we put a packing crate in the yard.

Some years before, we had purchased some old church windows at an auction — you just never know when you'll need something like that — and these became the inspiration for the design. Around these, we decided on a board-and-bat design with gables and a porch. I built the house with plywood and nailed vertical strips of wood (the bats) over the exterior. I used rounded cedar shingles for the roof. The interior has three levels all accessed by ladders. Lin painted the house in a three-color Victorian mode to blend well with the surrounding people-size structures.

I do believe the neighbors liked Kate's playhouse better than Kate did!

P.S. Later, Kate decided she needed a swing to look like a house, with a second level to climb up into. What could an indulgent father do but build one?❞

— *Jack Presbury*

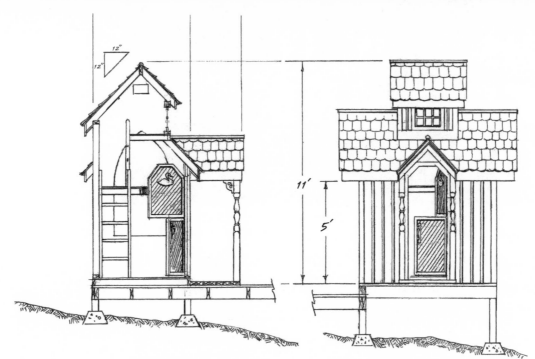

12"
12"
11'
5'

section view (left) and front elevation (right)

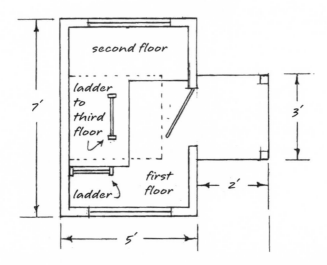

second floor

ladder to third floor

first floor

ladder

7'

3'

2'

5'

CHAPTER 6

BUILDING IT BIGGER AND BETTER

You thought you were done, right? Well, maybe you are. . . .
But say you have a lot of friends now, since clubhouses
seem to be powerful magnets, and you need more space.
Again, there are many possibilities. This chapter will
describe how to build inside walls and add on rooms.

Building an Inside Wall

A small room or alcove can be useful in a clubhouse. It's a place where you can
read or talk or hide from everything. You and your friends can create your own private places with an inside wall, also called a partition.

Sometimes building an inside wall might seem like a great idea, but once it's
up, it might make the clubhouse feel crowded, dark, or awkward. If you are not
sure you want a partition, try hanging an old blanket where your wall would be.

Mark the beams.

Plumb it up!

ALCOVE

marks

Check for plumb.

ROOM WITH DOORWAY

Build wall frames outside.

BUILD A SIMPLE PARTITION

You can build a simple partition by nailing 2×3 or 2×4 studs to the roof beams and to the floor, then nailing boards across the studs. Here's how:

Step 1. Decide how wide you want your new room to be.

Step 2. Measure along each roof beam from an existing wall, and make a mark on the beam. Measure the same distance along the floor and make another mark.

Step 3. Measure from the ceiling to the floor to find the length of the studs.

Step 4. Stand each stud on the floor, nail it to the roof beam by your mark, and use your level to make sure each stud is plumb before nailing it to the floor.

Step 5. Toenail the studs into the floor.

Step 6. Nail a stud against the wall where the partition will meet it, or use one of the studs already in the wall, if you haven't paneled it yet (see the drawing above).

Step 7. Nail boards to the studs, and you have your partition.

BUILD A WALL-FRAME PARTITION

If you have already paneled your inside walls or you want real inside walls, you can build partition frames outside, then bring them in and nail them in place.

Step 1. Decide on how big your inside room will be.

Step 2. Measure and mark the ceiling beams and the floor where the wall will go.

Step 3. Carefully measure the distance between the floor and the ceiling beams so you know how tall your partition frame should be. Also check to make sure the frames will fit through the door.

Step 4. Build each wall frame outside, then bring it inside. Set it to your marks and nail it to the ceiling beams, then use your level to make it all plumb (see the drawing on page 65).

Step 5. Nail the frame into the floor and into the walls.

Step 6. Add boards or paneling to one or both sides of the frame to close up your new room (see more about installing inside paneling on page 120).

Step 7. Hang a curtain over the doorway or build a door. Now you have an inner sanctum.

PARTITIONING POSSIBILITIES

6' x 8' Classic Clubhouse

Adding a Room

If your clubhouse becomes too small, you can add another room. To determine how big your addition should be, think about what you'll want to use it for. Then think about how it will attach to your original clubhouse. Is there room for it? Draw floor plans and maybe a picture of how you think the new room might look. Try different ideas. This could save a lot of extra work in the long run.

I'll describe a room that's 5 feet by 6 feet in size, but of course you can design a different size or shape. To build it this size, you will need your essential tools, a stepladder, and the materials listed on page 95.

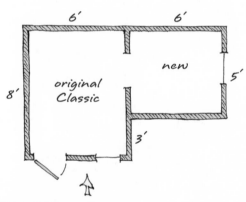

This is the plan we'll use as our example in the following instructions for adding on a room.

POSSIBILITIES FOR ADDING A ROOM

Materials for Adding a Room

Part	Quantity	Description
Sills	1	4×4, 10 feet long (to be cut in half)
Roof beams	1	2×6, 10 feet long (to be cut in half)
Joists, studs, and roof beams	28	2×4s, 6 feet long
Floorboards, wall sheathing, and roof boards	25	1×8 car siding boards, 12 feet long (pine boards, plywood, OSB, or other sheathing can be substituted)
Roof covering	1	roll mineral-coated roofing (better) or 30-pound felt underlayment (okay)
Brace and trim boards	8	1×3 or 1×4 furring strips, 8 feet long
Window	1	any size, with hinges and screws (optional)
Door	1	any size, with hinges and screws (optional)
Nails	2 pounds of each	12d or 16d coated sinkers; 6d or 8d coated sinkers
Nails	1 pound of each	6d galvanized box nails; ¾"- or 1"-long roofing nails

Kids Reality Check

Check with those in power before building an addition. You can casually mention that you and your friends are thinking of adding another room to your clubhouse . . . and see what kind of reaction you'll get. If they aren't sure about it, show them a drawing of what the addition might look like. Persist.

To help you with planning, on page 93 are some possible floor plans and drawings showing how an addition could connect to the Classic Clubhouse. To minimize the work needed to build a doorway, you can add the room to that part of your clubhouse where there is already a window or a door. You can then build a new door on your addition. Also, think about adding a window or two for more light and air or maybe an escape hatch. Otherwise, build the addition the same way you built your original clubhouse.

Building the Foundation

It's important that the new foundation be square to and level with the foundation of the existing clubhouse. Here's how to lay it out.

LAY OUT THE FOUNDATION

Step 1. Clear the ground and lay out a foundation where you want to build your new room. Measure out 6 feet from your clubhouse and 5 feet across, then drive stakes to mark your corners, as you did for your original clubhouse (see page 55).

Step 2. Check the stakes for square by measuring diagonally from corner to corner. At 6 feet by 5 feet, your new foundation will be square if your diagonal measurement is 93¾" in both directions.

Step 3. Lay cornerstones of concrete blocks or bricks at all four corners. Set them so they are level with those under your clubhouse, so that your new floor will be at the same height. If the ground slopes, then set your new cornerstones level to each other, and allow for a step up or down to your new room.

Building the Floor

Build the new floor with sills, joists, and floorboards as shown in chapter 3 (see pages 58–61).

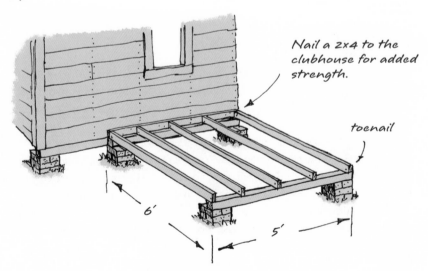

Nail a 2x4 to the clubhouse for added strength.

toenail

6'

5'

Making the Interior Doorway

Now would be a good time to make a doorway from your clubhouse to your new room. First comes deconstruction.

CUT A NEW DOORWAY

Step 1. If there is a window in the wall, take it out and saw off all the sheathing and paneling down to the floor below the old window. Watch for nails, and use a crowbar to pry out any blocking. If there is no window, take out one board, preferably at the top of your new doorway, and saw out a doorway along the side of two studs, all the way to the floor. You may have to remove a larger piece of plywood or OSB sheathing to begin sawing, then replace the scraps.

Step 2. Saw off the bottom plate that passes through the new doorway so you won't trip over it.

new foundation and floor

HOW TO FRAME A WIDE DOORWAY

If you want a wide opening through your clubhouse wall into your addition and you have to take out a stud or two, then you'll have to support the original wall with a beam called a header. This is the same kind of header you would put in over a big window (see page 164). Here's how to frame a wide opening to your new room.

Step 1. Remove the sheathing, studs, and bottom plate from the original wall. Leave the top plate in place.

Step 2. Cut two 2×4 trimmers to the height of your new opening, and nail them to the remaining original studs.

Step 3. Cut a header long enough to rest on the trimmers and fit snugly between the original studs. A 4×4 header will work fine, or you can make a header by nailing together two 2×4s with some scraps of ½"-thick plywood or OSB in between to make it the thickness of a wall.

Step 4. If there is room, add short 2×4 pieces called cripples above the header to support the top plate.

Step 5. Replace any sheathing you removed on the original wall (see the drawing below).

A Superwide Opening

If the opening into the addition is so wide that the header will be more than 5 feet long, use a solid 4×6, or two 2×6s and ½" plywood nailed together, for a header.

cripples

new
header
and
trimmers

existing
framing

existing
siding or
sheathing

bottom plate
cut away

← 8-foot existing wall →

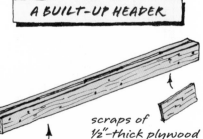

A BUILT-UP HEADER

scraps of
½"-thick plywood
or OSB

two 2x4s

FRAMING THE WALLS AND ROOF

Once your doorway is in and the floor is built, you'll need to frame three walls all the same height. Here you will need to think about the roof.

There are several ways you can tie the roof of your addition to the roof of the original clubhouse, depending on how high you want your new walls to be. You can add your new room to the lower end of your clubhouse, with the new roof continuing the slope of the old one. Or you can add your new room to the higher end of your clubhouse. You can join the new roof to the old roof at the peak or just enough below the peak (at least 9") to clear the overhang (see the drawings below). Any of these methods allows you to use the same roof-beam design described in chapter 4.

For our example, we'll join the new roof to the original roof at the peak of the Classic Clubhouse. We'll also build the new walls to the same height (5'6") as the walls in the Classic Clubhouse, using the same framing methods described in chapter 4.

ROOF VARIATIONS FOR AN ADDITION

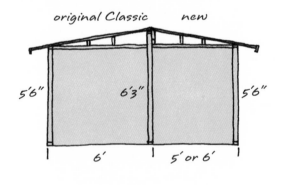

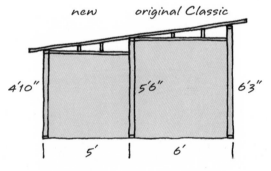

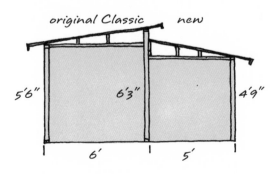

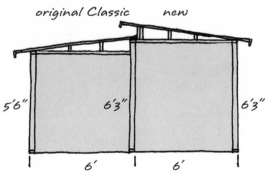

FRAME THE WALLS

Step 1. On your sawhorses, cut the top and bottom plates for the end wall exactly 5 feet (60″) long.

Step 2. With both plates set on edge together, measure every 20″ and draw centerlines for the studs. This measurement (instead of 24″ as used when framing the original walls) spreads the studs out evenly on this short wall, unless you have a wider door or window. (See chapter 4 again if you need help to frame in a door or windows.)

Step 3. Cut four more plates for the two side walls at 6 feet long minus the width of the plates of the end wall: 72″ – 3½″ = 68½″ long.

Step 4. Set all four of these plates on edge, then measure and draw centerlines at every 24″ for these studs.

Step 5. Cut 12 studs at 63″ long, which is the height of your wall minus the thickness of your top and bottom plates: 66″ – 3″ = 63″.

Step 6. On the ground, lay out the plates with the studs for the three new walls as shown in chapter 4 (see page 65).

Step 7. Nail each of the three new walls together, using 12d or 16d nails.

Step 8. Stand up the wall frames on your floor one at a time, check them with your level to make sure they are plumb, nail them to your floor, and brace them, as shown in chapter 4.

Step 9. Nail the corners together, and nail the side wall frames tightly to the side of your clubhouse (see the drawing below).

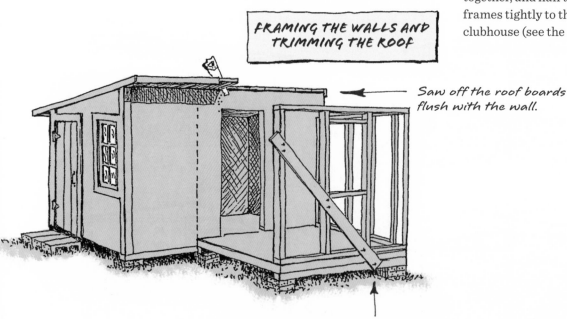

FRAMING THE WALLS AND TRIMMING THE ROOF

Saw off the roof boards flush with the wall.

temporary brace

TRIM THE ROOF OVERHANG

Next, you will want to saw off part of the original roof overhang so that the new roof and old roof will meet at a peak.

Step 1. Climb up on the roof, or up a stepladder. Bring your saw, hammer, crowbar, and utility knife, along with a straight board and a pencil.

Step 2. Pry off and peel back (as gently as possible) the original roofing. If it tears, don't worry about it; it's easy to repair. Then set your straight board over the roof and draw a cut line where the original roof overhang begins.

Step 3. Saw through the roof boards and roof trim boards until you are just above the new wall frame, as shown in the drawing on page 100.

FRAME THE ROOF

Now you can frame the roof. You'll need a stepladder and a helpful friend.

Step 1. On your sawhorses, cut a 2×4 and a 2×6 to 5 feet long.

Step 2. Set them on edge, one on top of the other, on top of your new wall frame against the clubhouse wall, then nail them both into the wall.

Step 3. Cut another 2×4 and another 2×6 to 5 feet long, and set them across the wall top plates, as shown in the drawing at right.

Step 4. Use a straight roof board, or your long level, to determine the proper spacing. The roof board should rest evenly on the new end-wall top plate, the 2×4, the 2×6, and the stacked 2×4 and 2×6 nailed to the clubhouse.

Step 5. When you have the spacing right, toenail the roof beams to the top of your walls with 6d nails.

stacked 2x4 and 2x6

end-wall top plate

2x6   2x4

FINISHING THE ROOM

Cover the walls and roof of your addition with car siding, boards, OSB, or plywood. Install any windows and doors, as shown in chapter 5. Add trim boards to the roof, the corners, and around your windows or door, and you are done. Then you can paint or add siding if you want to. (See the next chapter for siding details.)

Alternative: Building a Small Addition

If you'd rather add on a small hideaway room, this addition is for you. It uses the same method of construction as the larger addition just described, but it is 5 feet by 5 feet wide and the inside is at most 4 feet 9 inches tall. It is low enough to attach under the existing clubhouse roof, so you won't have to saw off the old roof overhang.

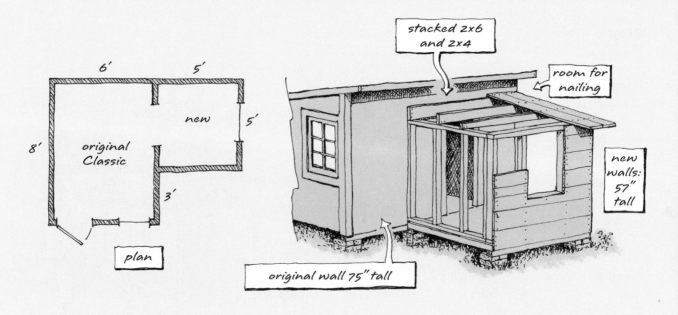

NAN'S ITALIANATE CUPOLA

This playhouse once graced the top of a Berlin, Wisconsin, Italianate-style house originally built in the 1860s. In 1938, the owner, Frank Betchkal, removed the cupola when renovating the house and set it in the yard for his daughter, Nan. He had a concrete foundation prepared and a door installed. Otherwise, the structure is preserved exactly as it was built 150 years ago.

Everett Caldwell bought the property in 1956, and his daughters, Carol and Barbara, used it as a place in which to "dress up and play house." Since these girls have grown, the playhouse has experienced a period of sedate retirement, patiently awaiting future generations.

CHAPTER 7

MAKING IT YOUR OWN

You've built your clubhouse! Now you might be hanging out and thinking, "This could look better. What could we do to make this place look more like *we* want it?" Well, you can fix up your clubhouse in a thousand different ways. The following pages suggest how you can decorate it on the outside and the inside, as well as fix up the outdoor space with a clubhouse garden or patio.

Fixing up can be a never-ending process for your clubhouse, simply because it's so much fun. Your results will depend on what materials you find and how creative you want to be. Once the door is on and your clubhouse is "closed up," as house builders say, you'll probably want to finish the outside first. This is an important step if uptight parents or neighbors have to look at it. You'll also feel proud of how great it will look, and a good-looking clubhouse will command respect; other kids will less likely trash it.

Trimming and Painting the Outside

If you haven't done so already, add some 1×3 or 1×4 trim boards around your windows and doors and on the wall corners. On the corners, extend the trim boards ½" *below* the bottom of the sheathing boards covering your clubhouse. This will help later when you put on finish siding. The trim boards cover all those little gaps you might have left and give the place a finished look. Now your clubhouse is ready for painting or adding siding of some kind.

The easiest way to decorate the outside is simply to paint it. One gallon of house paint should cover the outside of the Classic Clubhouse. If you have more than one paint color, play with ideas such as painting the trim boards a different color than the walls or painting one side a different color than the other. You're the designer.

Use water-based paint only. Water-based paints are labeled "latex," "latex enamel," or "acrylic-latex." The label might also say "flat," "eggshell," "satin," "semi-gloss," or "gloss." These terms indicate the texture of the paint when it's dry: Flat is really dull, gloss is really shiny, satin and semi-gloss are in between, and eggshell has the texture of, you guessed it, eggshells.

Painting is pretty easy, but it does take some practice to do it well. To start, get a good-quality paintbrush about 2½" to 3" wide for painting the walls. Also get a 1½"-wide angled brush called a beveled cutting brush for painting edges; a beveled brush is especially helpful where two colors meet or you have to paint against the glass on a window.

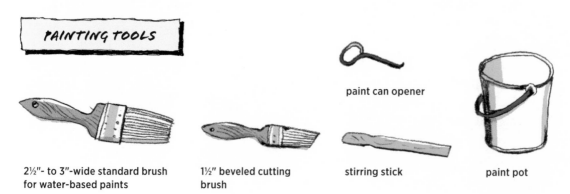

PAINTING TOOLS

paint can opener

2½"- to 3"-wide standard brush for water-based paints

1½" beveled cutting brush

stirring stick

paint pot

HOW TO PAINT

Step 1. Pry open a can of paint with a flat-head screwdriver or a paint can opener. Stir the paint thoroughly with a clean stick. If the can is more than half full, pour some paint into a smaller paint pot, to about half full or less, then put the lid back on the paint can. A smaller paint pot is easier to handle, and if it spills, you won't lose all your paint.

Step 2. Dip your brush into the pot, and smack a little off on the inside of the pot so it won't drip.

Step 3. Brush the paint onto the wall with a few long strokes to cover the wood, then work the brush into all the little cracks and holes, especially if the wood is old or rough.

Step 4. Reload your brush, and use long strokes over what you just covered. That will help make an even, smooth coat of paint with no drips or bare spots.

Step 5. Keep going. Eventually you'll find the right balance between too much and not enough paint on your brush, and you'll also find the best way to get the paint on the wall without dripping. As with most things, painting will get easier the more you practice.

Step 6. When you're done painting, dump the leftover paint back in the paint can, then brush all the paint remaining on the sides of the paint pot into the paint can. Reseal the paint can by tapping the lid firmly with your hammer or the side of a 2×4 block.

Step 7. To clean up, fill the paint pot with warm water with a little dish soap, and stick your brush in it for an hour or more to help soak out the paint. Later, rinse the brush in warm water until the water running through it comes out clear — then you'll know your brush is clean. Tap the brush or use a rag to get out the excess water. If the brush came wrapped in a cardboard folder, put it back in the folder to keep the bristles straight. Rinse out the paint pot, and you're done.

Avoid Oil Paints

If a well-meaning friend or neighbor gives you oil-based paint or, worse, auto-body or other industrial paints for your clubhouse, don't use them! They are poisonous and they need toxic solvents to clean the brushes.

Installing Siding

If you have the itch to keep building, you might get lucky and find (or be able to buy) some shingles, clapboards, car siding, board-and-batten, or other wood siding for your clubhouse. These are the safest and easiest kinds of siding to put up, requiring only hand tools. Finish siding can make your clubhouse look very good indeed.

I don't recommend vinyl siding (that plastic stuff you see on newer houses everywhere in America) because special tools are needed to work with it. The same goes for any siding made of aluminum, steel, fiber-cement board, or heavy plywood siding, such as T1-11.

SIDING STYLES FOR A CLUBHOUSE

shingles

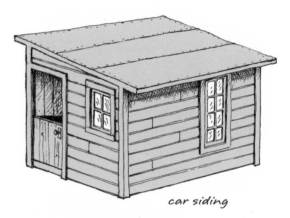
car siding

board-and-batten

clapboard

Siding with Shingles

Shingles have been used to cover houses for hundreds of years. They are thin, tapered strips of wood (usually cedar) about 16″ long and from 2″ to 10″ wide. The thicker bottom end of a shingle is called the butt. Shingles are graded like lumber from no. 1 to no. 3 and are sold in bundles. I recommend no. 3 or "backup" shingles for their low cost and wide availability. Shingles are quite easy to put on, and after a while, you'll understand the logic of how they shed water. You will need your hammer, a 1-pound box of 3d galvanized box nails, a utility knife, and a handsaw.

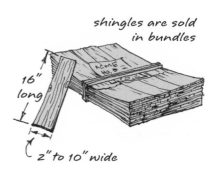

shingles are sold in bundles

16″ long

2″ to 10″ wide

Housewrap

Most builders put tar paper or, nowadays, a special white plastic called "housewrap" on house walls before nailing on the siding, which helps keep the inside dry. Shingles, clapboards, or other siding will do a good job by themselves, especially for a clubhouse, so it is your choice on that one. If you have tar paper (not the mineral-coated kind) left over from your roof, save money and use that.

HOW TO SHINGLE

Step 1. To start, temporarily nail or prop up a straight board at the bottom of the wall so the top of the board is ½″ below the bottom of the sheathing boards. This will be your guide for nailing the first two rows, or courses, of shingles. (I'm assuming you've put the trim boards on the corners by now because the shingles will be nailed up against the trim board edges.)

Step 2. Load up your nail apron with 3d nails.

Step 3. Grab a wide shingle and set it on your guide board and against the corner trim board.

Step 4. Drive a nail about 7″ above the bottom of the shingle and ¾″ in from each shingle edge. No matter how wide the shingle is, use only two nails per shingle.

continued on next page

The bottom row of shingles is doubled to protect against water infiltration.

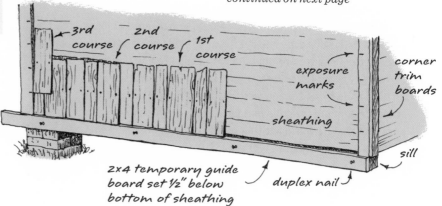

3rd course   2nd course   1st course

exposure marks

corner trim boards

sheathing

sill

2x4 temporary guide board set ½″ below bottom of sheathing

duplex nail

Step 5. Add more shingles, mixing narrow and wide ones in a random pattern, as shown in the drawing on page 109.

Step 6. As you nail the second course of shingles over the first one, stagger the shingles by keeping the vertical joints or cracks between shingles at least 1" away from those on the row of shingles beneath.

Step 7. Continue nailing both rows all the way to the other end of the wall, as shown in the drawing on page 109.

Step 8. When you get to the far end, set the last shingle against the trim board, and mark its top and bottom with your pencil so you can cut it to fit.

Step 9. Get out your utility knife. Set the edge of a straight piece of wood on the shingle at the two marks, and pull your knife along the piece of wood to cut the shingle. This works well until you hit a knot; if this happens, use your saw to cut the shingle. Be careful with the knife — it is sharp!

Step 10. Next, measure up from the bottom of both trim boards, and make pencil marks every 6" (6", 12", 18", 24", and so on). This will mark the exposure of your shingles. House builders will call this "6 inches to the weather." These marks will tell you where the bottoms of every row of shingles will be.

Step 11. Start the next row of shingles at the corner board. Line up the bottom of a shingle with the mark you made on the corner board, check the vertical edge to make sure it is not over the crack between the shingles below, and nail it in. Add more shingles in the same way.

Keeping Courses Straight

To keep your rows of shingles straight, there are two methods:

- **GUIDE BLOCK.** For short walls, and most clubhouses, you can use a guide block. This is an easy-to-make piece of ¾"-thick wood with a 6"-long notch cut into one side. Simply hold the block so the notch is hooked on a shingle you have already nailed in, then set the shingle you want to nail on the top of the block. Remove the block and nail in your shingle.
- **CHALK LINE.** For long walls, you can use a chalk line, which is a long string with a little hook at the end that is kept inside a "chalk box" filled with bright blue or red chalk. Hook the string to a small nail (or have a helper hold it) at the exposure marks on both ends of the shingle row, and pull it tight. Then pull the string straight out from the middle of the wall and let it snap back; the chalk leaves a line that is your guide for aligning the bottoms of the shingles.

HOW TO SHINGLE AROUND A WINDOW

When you get to a window, you'll have to trim the shingles to fit around it.

Step 1. Set the first shingle to be cut over the window trim, and hold it steady while you mark where it needs to be cut.

Step 2. On your sawhorse, first cut across the grain of the shingle with your saw. Then switch to a utility knife to cut with the grain, as before. This lessens the chance of splitting the shingle.

Step 3. Nail the shingle in place.

Step 4. Cut the remaining short shingles that go under the window to the same length with your saw. If these are shorter than 4", use a trim board instead. The same method applies when you get to the top of your wall.

If you goof while installing a shingle, you can use your crowbar to pry off the shingle. Pound the short leg of the crowbar under the shingle at the nail head and then pry. You might lose part of the shingle (they split easily), but the middle might still be good enough to reuse.

guide block

If you goof, pry up the nails and try again.

Siding with Clapboard or Beveled Siding

Clapboard, which is also called beveled siding, is somewhat easier and faster to put on than shingles. Clapboards are set against the corner trim boards, just as shingles. They are usually 6″ or 8″ wide, about ½″ thick at the butt (the bottom edge), and *beveled,* or tapered, to about ⅛″ thick at the top edge. The 6″-wide clapboards are better for the scale of a clubhouse.

The standard exposure of wood to weather for 6″-wide clapboard is 4½″. Some clapboard styles have a special ledge, or "rabbet," in the back that guides your exposure for you. If not, make a guide block that is set for a 4½″ exposure, as described on page 110.

A Note on Scale

In architecture, scale is the idea of using the right-size objects or patterns to fit a certain size of building. A smaller-size clubhouse needs smaller-size doors and windows, as well as small-patterned finishes like shingles and skinny clapboards, to give it the right scale.

HOW TO PUT UP CLAPBOARDS

Putting up clapboards takes a lot of nailing, so put on your nail apron and load it up with 6d galvanized box nails.

Step 1. Set a long, straight clapboard at the bottom of the sheathing. Have a friend help hold it there. If one end overlaps the corner trim board, use a pencil to mark the point where the clapboard meets the inside edge of the trim board. Then take the clapboard to your sawhorses, draw a cut line at the mark using your square, and saw off the scrap. (Alternatively, instead of using a pencil, you can draw, or score, the cut line with your utility knife to help guide your saw for a clean cut.)

Step 2. Bring the clapboard back to the wall, and set it against the sheathing so that it overhangs the bottom of the sheathing by ½″. Have a friend help you hold it while you tack it in place with a nail or two.

Step 3. Drive a nail every 16″ to 24″ along the board, about 1″ up from the butt. If you can, drive the nails into the studs beneath the sheathing, so they won't poke through on the inside. When you get to the end of a clapboard, drive a nail 1″ to 2″ from the end. And as you work, keep each clapboard end at least 6″ away from a joint in any adjoining course.

Step 4. When you've finished the first row, or course, of clapboard, it's time to mark the location of the remaining courses on the corner trim boards, so you can align the clapboards evenly. For 6″-wide clapboards, 4½″ of each course is exposed. Measuring up from the bottom of the corner trim boards, mark the courses, at 4½″, 9″, 13½″, and so on, to set the bottom edge (or butt) of the clapboards. Then make a guide block similar to the one for shingles, but set for 4½″ of exposure instead of 6″ (see page 110).

Step 5. Set each clapboard to the marks on the corner trim boards, and, using your guide block, nail it in.

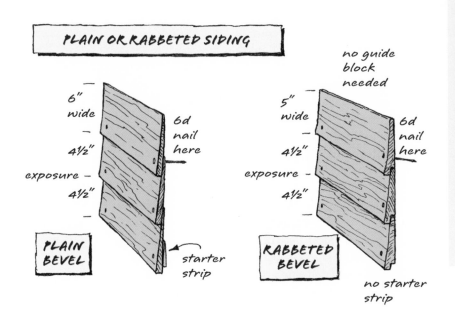

PLAIN OR RABBETED SIDING

6" wide

4½" exposure

4½"

PLAIN BEVEL

6d nail here

starter strip

no guide block needed

5" wide

4½" exposure

4½"

RABBETED BEVEL

6d nail here

no starter strip

A Starter Strip

For a professional look with clapboards, nail on a starter strip at the bottom of the wall first. The starter strip will hold the first clapboard at the same angle as the clapboards above it. Cut a 1½"-wide strip off a clapboard's upper edge, and nail that with some 3d galvanized box nails along the very bottom of the sheathing (not ½" below it). Then set the first clapboard over the strip and ½" below the sheathing, and nail it in.

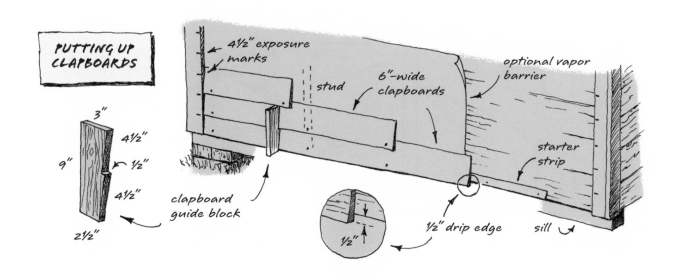

PUTTING UP CLAPBOARDS

3"

9"

4½"

½"

4½"

2½"

clapboard guide block

4½" exposure marks

stud

6"-wide clapboards

optional vapor barrier

starter strip

½" drip edge

sill

½"

HOW TO INSTALL CLAPBOARD AROUND A WINDOW

When you get to the bottom of a window, you'll have to cut away some wood to fit around the window trim boards. This isn't difficult, but it takes some patience.

Step 1. Set the clapboard over the window trim, as shown below, and use a pencil to mark the part that needs to be cut out.

Step 2. On your sawhorses, saw the vertical edges of the notch to the corners.

Step 3. To cut along the horizontal line, get your hammer and a chisel. Use a clamp or have a friend hold down the clapboard. Hold the chisel's cutting edge on the line, with the flat side to the good part of your board, and hit it hard enough with your hammer to cut through the wood. Keep chiseling along the horizontal line until the scrap breaks off. Watch the grain of the wood so your cut doesn't break into the good part. If it starts to do that, go to the other end and chisel the other way.

Step 4. If you are cutting out a long piece, use your handsaw to finish the job once you have some room. You can also use your utility knife and a long steel ruler to cut through it if the wood is thin enough and there are no knots.

Mark the edges of the window trim.

CUT OUT THE SCRAP

Use a clamp.

Watch the grain.

Chisel on a heavy board.

HOW TO INSTALL CLAPBOARD AT THE TOP OF A WALL

When you get to the top of the wall, you can simply stop. If there is a gap between the last clapboard and the roof overhang, cover it with a trim board. The remaining clapboard left over from your starter strip might fit up there if you're lucky. If the top of the wall is slanted, you'll have to cut the clapboard to fit:

Step 1. Mark the ends of the clapboards where they overlap the trim board at the roof.

Step 2. Connect the marks with a cut line, and saw off the scrap.

If the roof overhangs too far to mark the clapboard, measure from the point where the clapboard hits the overhang to the same point of the clapboard below. Then draw a line between the marks and saw off the scrap. If you need to carve off a bit more wood, try using your utility knife.

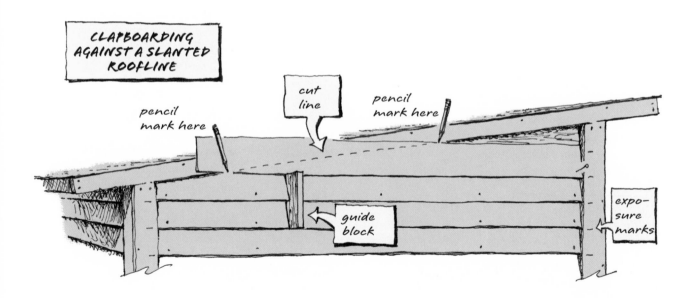

Siding with Car Siding

Named for their original use for lining the inside walls of railway cars, pine car-siding boards are ¾" thick and 6" or 8" wide, and they are tongue-and-grooved for a tight fit. Car siding boards usually have V-grooves on one side and are smooth and flat on the other.

As I mentioned in chapter 5, car siding is strong enough to use as sheathing and finish siding, and it is relatively inexpensive. If you have to buy sheathing and you like the look of car siding as a finish siding, save time and money by just using car siding. Use it smooth side up for a strong floor and roof as well.

car siding

1x8   1x6

HOW TO INSTALL CAR SIDING

To install car siding as sheathing and finish siding, you'll cover one wall at a time, while leaving the brace boards up on the other walls. For strong walls, measure and cut each board so its ends are set over studs.

Step 1. Start the first board ½" below the bottom of the floor joists for all the walls (see the drawing on facing page). Making sure the tongue is at the top of the board, have a friend help hold the board, and nail it in with 6d or 8d galvanized box nails. Use at least two nails at each end of the board and two nails over each stud.

JOINING A STUBBORN BOARD

grooved scrap

Step 2. Fit the groove of the second board firmly over the tongue of the first one. If they don't join tightly, look in the groove for anything stuck in there. If they still resist joining, use a scrap of wood as a hammer block and pound the boards together (see the drawing below left). Then nail the second board in place.

Step 3. Continue nailing on boards as described above. When you get to a door or window opening, measure and cut the boards carefully so you can nail them tightly and neatly against the framing. You can be less careful on the corners because the corner trim boards will cover up any small gaps.

Step 4. When you get to the top of the wall, measure the space needed for the last board, mark the board with your pencil and a long straightedge (a long, straight board will do), and then rip it with your saw. To "rip" means to saw a board along its length. This can take a while, so use clamps or have a friend help hold the board steady and also help you saw it.

Step 5. When all the car siding is nailed on, install the trim boards on the corners and around the windows as you would with rough sheathing.

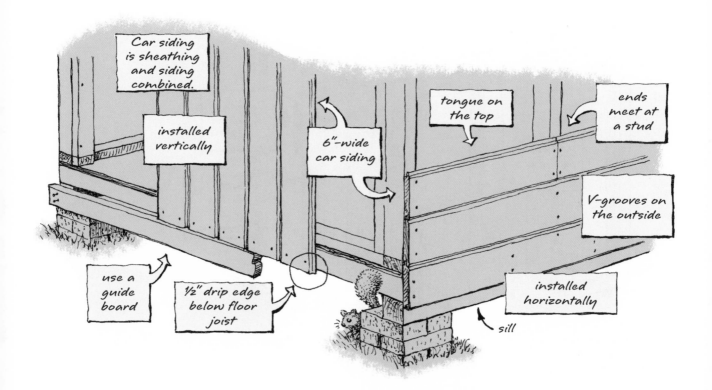

Car siding is sheathing and siding combined.

installed vertically

6"-wide car siding

tongue on the top

ends meet at a stud

V-grooves on the outside

use a guide board

½" drip edge below floor joist

installed horizontally

sill

Siding with Board-and-Batten

Board-and-batten, or board-and-bat as it's sometimes called, is another style of siding that can double as sheathing. This method uses plain, wide, ¾"-thick boards installed vertically. The joints between the boards are then covered with narrow boards or strips about 1½" wide, called battens or bats.

Old shed, barn, and fence boards — or any boards wider than 5" — will work well for board-and-batten. For battens, use 1×2 furring strips.

HOW TO INSTALL BOARD-AND-BATTEN

Cut the boards and bats long enough so they reach from the top plate to ½" below the bottom of the floor joists. Save any short boards for under the windows or over the door. For slanted walls, cut the tops of the boards at the same angle as the roof. To do this, hold the board in place and mark the angled edge of the roofline on the board with your pencil. Use your square to draw the cut line, then saw off the scrap.

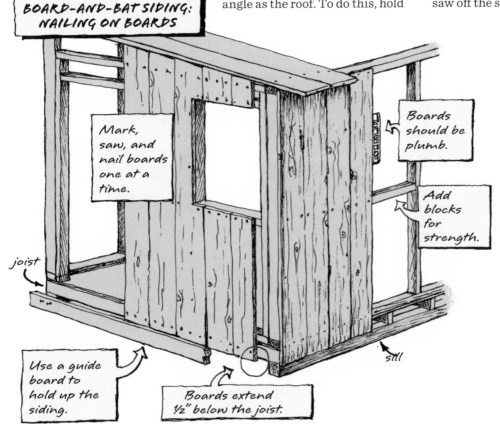

BOARD-AND-BAT SIDING:
NAILING ON BOARDS

Mark, saw, and nail boards one at a time.

Boards should be plumb.

Add blocks for strength.

joist

Use a guide board to hold up the siding.

Boards extend ½" below the joist.

sill

Step 1. Add a 2×4 block horizontally between each pair of studs, halfway between the top and bottom plates. These will strengthen the board-and-bat wall.

Step 2. Starting at a corner, nail the boards to the middle blocks and the plates, using three 8d galvanized box nails at each end and two in the middle. If a board rests over a stud, nail it into the stud every 16" or so. Use your level to check the boards once in a while to make sure they are plumb; they can get crooked.

Step 3. When the walls are covered with boards, nail on all your trim boards on the corners and around the door and windows *before* you nail on the bats. You can use extra bats as trim boards if they are wide enough.

Step 4. Nail on a top trim board where the wall meets the underside of the roof.

Step 5. Nail on all the vertical bats with 4d galvanized box nails, spacing the nails every 16".

BOARD-AND-BAT SIDING: TRIM AND BATTENS

1x3 trim

1x2 bat

Nail on trim boards, **THEN** the battens.

Fixing Up the Inside

As you fix up the outside, you're probably thinking of ways to fix up the inside as well. Your results will again depend on what materials you'll find and also how "houselike" you want your clubhouse to be. You can be creative with wallpaper, curtains, pictures, posters, signs, paneling, and, of course, paint. Garage sales are great places to find clubhouse-size tables, cabinets, chairs, knickknack shelves, pictures, fancy light fixtures, and whatever else might work.

Paneling the Inside Walls

If you want to finish the inside of your clubhouse with some kind of paneling, you will need to add some 2×4s, called nailers, to the inside corners so that you have something to nail the paneling to. Find or cut some 2×4 blocks about 12" long, and nail them against the corner studs, as shown in the drawing below. Then cut a new stud the same length as the one in the corner and nail that in. Now you have a surface on which to nail the outer edge of your paneling.

NAILER STUDS FOR INSIDE CORNERS

At an inside corner, only one wall has accessible framing to nail the paneling to.

So, add 2x4 blocks . . .

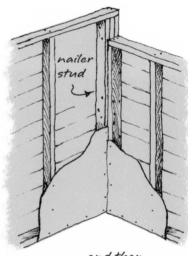

. . . and then a nailer stud.

Paneling Options

For paneling your walls, I recommend using anything made of wood. Thin boards that fit together tongue-and-groove style, called bead boards, are good for paneling, but any smooth boards will do. Many styles of interior wall paneling are made of thin fiberboard or plywood covered with printed designs or painted, but this stuff can be expensive, as well as difficult to put up. A far cheaper alternative is ¼"-thick OSB, whose finished side is smooth enough to paint or apply wallpaper.

You can also use drywall, otherwise known as wallboard, gypsum board, or Sheetrock, but it is heavy to lift, requires plastering skills to finish, and can get moldy if your clubhouse is in a shady or damp place. If you still want to use drywall, see page 212.

Painting the Inside

A good way to start is to paint your inside walls. You can paint them all the same color or as many different colors as you can acquire. You can mark up a wall with graffiti or paint a comic character, a superhero, or a mural. This is your place to experiment! For a cavelike den, use dark colors. If you don't like the results, you can always repaint. For more on how to paint, see page 107.

If you don't want to bother putting up paneling to paint, you can always just paint the studs and rough inside wood of your sheathing.

Wallpapering

If the interior paneling is ugly, you can paint it or cover it with wallpaper. Someone in your neighborhood might have some old wallpaper to give you, or you might be able to pick some up cheap at a rummage sale or a recycled building materials store.

If you want to try wallpapering, set up a table or some wide, clean boards on your sawhorses for cutting and gluing the paper, if necessary. You'll need a tape measure, scissors, a pencil, a long ruler, a level, a plastic tray and bucket for holding water, a wallpaper spreader (which is a wide, stiff brush), a clean rag, a utility knife, and a sponge. Check to see if your wallpaper is preglued (it will say on the label). If it's not, you'll also need wallpaper paste and a 4"-wide or wider brush for applying the paste.

Wallpaper is always hung vertically, and it's amazing how it can transform a room. Be patient with it, and take your time. (And see the step-by-step instructions on the next page.)

WALLPAPERING TOOLS & SUPPLIES

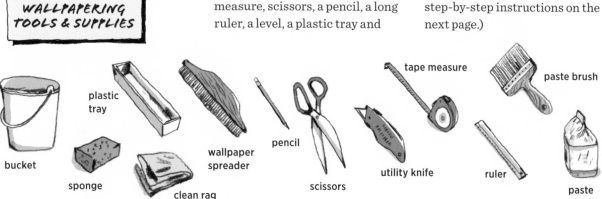

bucket · plastic tray · sponge · clean rag · wallpaper spreader · pencil · scissors · utility knife · tape measure · ruler · paste brush · paste

HOW TO INSTALL WALLPAPER

Step 1. Measure the distance from the floor to the ceiling of the wall you want to paper, and add an extra 4″ for trimming the wallpaper.

Step 2. With scissors, cut to size enough pieces of wallpaper to cover the wall.

Step 3. Using your pencil, a level, and a long ruler, draw a vertical line on the wall near the corner, which will be an edge mark for your first sheet of wallpaper. Or simply use the wall corner itself as your edge guide.

Step 4. If your wallpaper is preglued, fill a long, plastic tray (available at paint stores) with water. Soak the back of the wallpaper in the water, then put it up on the wall, being aware that some designs need to be right side up and match on the edges.

Step 5. If the paper is not preglued, mix wallpaper paste according to the instructions. Spread your wallpaper sheet facedown on the table, then paste the back of the paper using the big paste brush. Hold the sheet up to the wall and stick it on.

Step 6. If you have a wallpaper spreader, use it to smooth out the paper on the wall. A soft, clean rag will work as well.

Step 7. Tuck the ends of the paper neatly against the floor, the ceiling, and into the corners with a ruler or a paint-stirring stick. Then, with a sharp utility knife, cut away the extra paper from the top and bottom. The glue or paste can be messy but washes off easily; use a damp sponge to mop up the excess.

Step 8. When the first sheet is up, trimmed, and cleaned off, hold up the next one to match the design's edges, if necessary, then put it up the same way. Continue until all sheets are hung.

Finishing the Floor

Once you have finished painting, paneling, or papering the walls, you can finish your floor. If you have a smooth floor such as OSB, you can paint it by applying a base coat or primer coat on the raw wood, then a finish coat. Although water-based primers are the best for raw wood, you can save money and use almost any flat latex paint for a base coat. Don't use glossy paint for a base coat because the finish coat might not stick well to it. For a durable finish coat, use "porch and floor" acrylic enamel over the primer. Mix up colors and create designs if you want.

If your floor is made of rough boards, cover it with carpet scraps or an area rug. If the carpet is too big, measure the floor with your tape measure, then use your utility knife and a straight board to cut off the extra carpet. It can be tough to cut, so flip the carpet over and cut through the backing. Be patient and cut several times if necessary. Carpet pieces can be stuck to the floor with carpet tape or with old-fashioned carpet nails.

Now you're ready to move in!

Landscaping the Clubhouse Area

Another way to score points with those in power and to have fun with gardening and such is to fix up the ground or yard in front of your clubhouse. Some ideas:

- Make a walkway out from the door with bricks or stone pavers.
- Build a trellis.
- Build a rock garden with rocks, driftwood, and a variety of plants.
- Put in a pumpkin or veggie patch.
- Plant flowers, bushes, or trees.

Someone you know might have some old bricks or other pavers you can use. Your parents or neighbors might have seeds, geranium cuttings, iris bulbs, or other plants from their gardens that you can use. Fair warning: Don't dig up anyone's plants without asking first.

Laying a Brick Step

A simple brick step in front of your doorway is a good start. Find or buy bricks, colored concrete paver blocks, or even flat stones. You'll also need some plain, dry sand to help hold these in place. Other supplies and tools needed for laying brick or pavers include a tape measure, string, some wooden stakes about 12″ long, a shovel, a garden trowel, a short 2×4 or 1×4, a rubber mallet, and an old broom. You might also need a wheelbarrow to remove the dirt you dig up and to bring in the sand.

It's easy to build a brick step or walk in front of your clubhouse door. If you need a higher step to your door, you can set a row of three or four large stones, concrete blocks, or concrete cinder blocks at the door, in addition to your walkway.

TWO PATTERNS FOR BRICKWORK

basket weave

running bond

COMMON LANDSCAPE PAVERS

concrete brick

clay brick

concrete paver tiles

natural stone

HOW TO LAY A BRICK STEP

Step 1. Measure a 2-foot by 3-foot (or larger) rectangle, using stakes and strings to mark the edges. To avoid having to cut bricks or pavers, you can first lay out your bricks to the shape you want as a "dry run." Then mark its corners with stakes, and remove all the bricks.

Step 2. In your marked-out rectangle, dig out the grass and loose dirt to about 3" down, depending on the thickness of your pavers.

Step 3. Remove the stakes and string as you dig, since they have done their job.

Step 4. Next, dump in some sand and spread it out so it is about 1" deep. Use a short 2×4 or 1×4 to spread the sand and make it flat and even. This will be the base that you'll lay your bricks on.

Step 5. Lay down the bricks or pavers snugly together. If you use bricks, the patterns known as basket weave or running bond work well (see the drawing on page 123). Running bond allows you to use broken bricks as well as whole ones.

Step 6. Tap the bricks or pavers with a rubber mallet or the end of your hammer handle to set them evenly with their neighbors. You can also tamp them down with the edge of the short board you used for spreading the sand.

Step 7. When you've laid the bricks where you want them, sprinkle some dry sand all over the bricks, and sweep it back and forth with a broom to settle it into the cracks. Pack sand or soil up against the outside edges of your new step, and you're done.

string to guide digging

sand

Dig out dirt 3" to 4" deep.

sand base

HOW TO LAY A RAISED BRICK STEP

If the step needs to be a bit higher off the ground, add a frame of 2×4s around the edge to hold the bricks together. Here's how:

Step 1. Scrape away weeds and loose dirt.

Step 2. Lay your bricks out in a "dry run" as described on page 125, then measure the short sides of the rectangle.

Step 3. Cut two 2×4s 1″ longer than the measurement.

Step 4. Set these alongside the outside edge of the bricks, then measure the long sides plus the thickness of your two short 2×4s.

Step 5. Cut two more 2×4s the length of those measurements.

Step 6. Nail the 2×4s together with 12d or 16d nails to make a frame.

Step 7. Place the frame around your bricks; it should fit fine.

Step 8. Next, drive in some 12″-long 1×2 or 1×3 stakes against the 2×4s, and nail them to the 2×4s with some galvanized 6d nails to hold the frame in place.

Step 9. Remove the bricks from the frame, then fill the inside of the frame to within 2″ of the top with sand.

Step 10. Replace the bricks, and gently tamp them down.

Step 11. Sprinkle some dry sand all over the bricks, and sweep it back and forth to settle it into the cracks and alongside the frame. You're done!

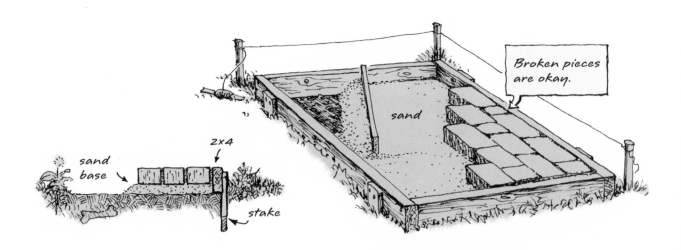

Building a Patio Trellis

A patio trellis provides a nice, shady spot next to your clubhouse. All you need is a trellis frame and something to cover it with. For a trellis 8 feet wide, you'll need the following:

Patio Trellis Materials

Part	Quantity	Description
Posts	2	2×4s or 4×4s, 8 feet long, pressure-treated
Beam	1	2×6, 8 feet long
Nailer	1	2×4, 8 feet long
Crosspieces	9	2×2 furring strips, 8 feet long
Nails	1 pound	12d or 16d galvanized box nails

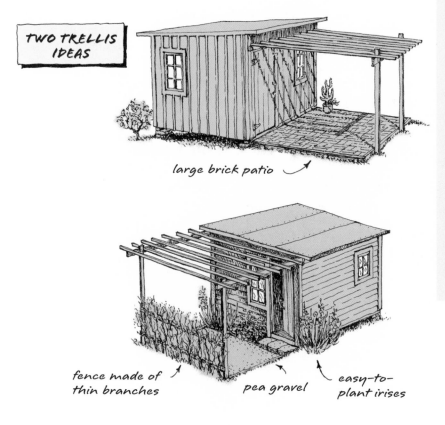

TWO TRELLIS IDEAS

large brick patio

fence made of thin branches

pea gravel

easy-to-plant irises

Patio Options

For a larger brick patio for your clubhouse, you can use the same method as you did to build the brick step. As an estimating guide, you'll need about six bricks for every square foot of patio.

You can also cover the ground with a layer of wood chips or small stones, called pea gravel, which is used in garden walkways. Prepare the ground as you would for a brick patio, then put down a layer of landscape fabric, a tough, weed-barrier cloth that is sold in rolls at garden-supply centers. Use bricks, stones, or boards for the edges, then fill the patio area with gravel or wood chips. Place stepping-stones in the chips or gravel for a walkway, if you desire.

However, if the ground drops off and you want a level patio, a wooden deck may be your best choice. Refer to the room-addition section in chapter 6, and build your deck as a stand-alone floor, without walls. Use cedar or pressure-treated pine posts, beams, and deck boards for a long-lasting deck.

HOW TO BUILD A TRELLIS

Step 1. Measure 6 feet out from each front corner of your clubhouse, and drive a stake in the ground. The stakes should be 8 feet apart. Check the positions of the stakes by measuring the diagonals, or the distance from each corner of the clubhouse to the opposite stake, which should be 10 feet. Next, measure 16″ in from each stake, toward the other stake; these spots mark your post holes (see the drawing below).

Step 2. Dig the holes about 2 feet deep. Drop in the posts and tamp dirt firmly around each one, while a friend uses a level to make sure each post is plumb.

Step 3. To mark the locations for your 2×2 trellis crosspieces, lay an 8-foot 2×6 and an 8-foot 2×4 side by side on your sawhorses. With your

tape measure and pencil, make a centerline mark every 12″ along the top edge of both boards. You should have seven marks, plus the ends, for the nine trellis crosspieces. Set the 2×6 aside.

Step 4. Turn the 2×4 flat, then pound a 12d or 16d galvanized box nail every foot or so *almost* all the way through the wide face of the 2×4, to get it ready to nail into the clubhouse.

Step 5. Have a friend or two hold the 2×4 against the clubhouse, with the mark edge facing up, well below the roof overhang but high enough overhead so no one will bang his or her head on the trellis, while you check it with your level. Once it's level, drive in the nails you have started while your helpers hold the board in place.

Step 6. Get the 2×6, and make a mark across it 16″ in from each end. Hold it up to the posts to make sure the marks are centered over the posts.

Step 7. Put the 2×6 back on the sawhorses, and pound in three or four 12d galvanized box nails *almost* all the way through it, along each of the two lines.

Step 8. Ask your friend to help hold the beam up to the posts. (For a good-looking trellis, the 2×6 should either be level with or lower than the 2×4 on the clubhouse. This beam can be quite low if it's not over a walkway.) Standing on a stepladder, pound *one* of the nails into a post, then move the ladder to the next post.

Step 9. Place your level on top of the beam, and slide the beam up or down until it is level. While your friend holds the beam steady, nail all the nails into the second post, then do the same into the first post. Be patient: The whole thing will wiggle a lot, but try to get the nails all the way in. If some get bent, nail in more. Hit 'em harder!

STARTING A TRELLIS

6′

6′

5′8″

Step 10. Decide whether you want to leave the trellis cross-pieces the full 8 feet long or trim them shorter; it's your choice. Using a ladder, set a 2×2 over a centerline mark on the 2×4 nailed to the clubhouse and on the beam you just put up. Nail the 2×2 to the 2×4 with a single 8d or 12d galvanized box nail but not yet into the beam.

You might have to toenail it into the clubhouse wall if the roof is in the way.

Step 11. Repeat this with the other 2×2 pieces, nailing them only into the 2×4.

Step 12. Next, check the posts to see if they are still plumb. If so,

nail the 2×2 nearest the post into the top of the 2×6 beam on the centerline mark.

Step 13. Do this again near the other post, then nail the rest of the 2×2s into the beam over the centerline marks, each with a single 8d or 12d galvanized box nail.

PUTTING UP THE TRELLIS BEAM

marks for trellis pieces

2×4 nailer

2×6 beam

HOW TO BUILD A TRELLIS OFF THE ROOF

If you have a smaller clubhouse, you can attach a good-looking trellis to the top of the roof, as shown in the drawing below. Here's how:

Step 1. Mark a 6-foot-long 2×4 and a 2×6 with centerline marks every 12″.

Step 2. Measure 6 feet out from the front of the clubhouse, and put in the two posts as described on page 128.

Step 3. Set the beam lower than the roof height, but keep adequate headroom where people will walk. Have a friend help you level it and nail it to the posts.

Step 4. On your sawhorses, drive six or more 8d or 12d galvanized nails almost through the marked-up 2×4.

Step 5. Lay the 2×4 flat on the top edge of the clubhouse roof, and drive in the nails. It might bounce a bit, so be patient.

Step 6. Set your trellis pieces (you'll need seven this time). Nail them first into the 2×4 on the roof, then into the beam after the posts have been plumbed, as described above. This trellis method can also be used on any other clubhouse.

A TRELLIS OFF THE ROOF

2x4 nailed to roof

2x2 trellis pieces

2x6 beam

string for peas or beans

fence if you want

FINISHING YOUR TRELLIS

Split-bamboo fencing will work great to cover your trellis and give you lots of shade. It is lightweight and inexpensive, and it holds up to the weather. Another good covering is a piece of canvas, burlap, or other sturdy fabric. Staple or tack it down well so the wind won't wreck it. To add some plants, you can use strings to train vines to grow up to the trellis. The trellis will also look fine with nothing at all.

Now you can set up a chair under your trellis, relax, and think about what kind of garden you might like to have.

Starting a Garden

It is curiously wonderful to watch flowers, bushes, vines, and trees that you have planted grow. What you plant depends in large part on how much space you have and what sort of sunlight it gets. Pumpkins, sweet corn, and beans grow very fast but need a large, sunny growing space. (You can grow all three together if you want, just like Native American tribes did.) Climbing beans, peas, and annual flowers such as nasturtiums need less room.

For faster results, start with transplants or cuttings — pieces of bigger plants that have been cut off or dug up and will grow into entirely new plants. Geraniums, hostas, and many other perennial plants are easy to dig up and start in a new garden. In the fall, plant iris, tulip, or daffodil bulbs, which are like large seeds, and watch them grow the following spring.

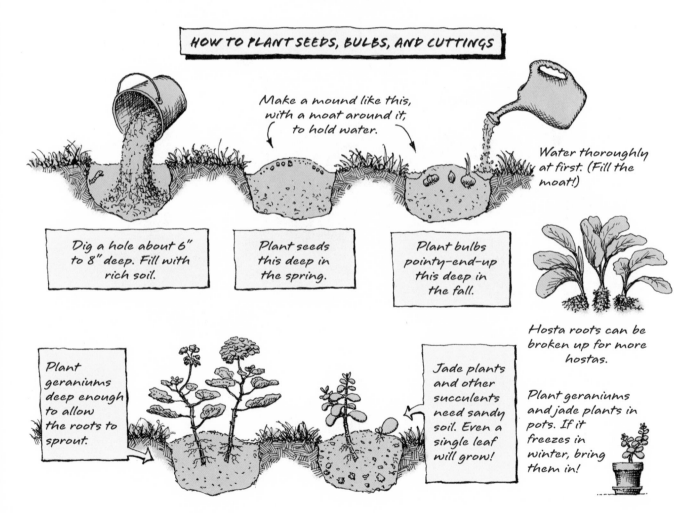

HOW TO PLANT SEEDS, BULBS, AND CUTTINGS

Make a mound like this, with a moat around it, to hold water.

Water thoroughly at first. (Fill the moat!)

Dig a hole about 6" to 8" deep. Fill with rich soil.

Plant seeds this deep in the spring.

Plant bulbs pointy-end-up this deep in the fall.

Hosta roots can be broken up for more hostas.

Plant geraniums deep enough to allow the roots to sprout.

Jade plants and other succulents need sandy soil. Even a single leaf will grow!

Plant geraniums and jade plants in pots. If it freezes in winter, bring them in!

Building a Rock Garden

If there are rocks or fieldstones nearby, you can use them for the edge of your patio, for around a garden, or for creating a miniature mountain. Driftwood works well, too. Set the rocks where you want them, then plant some perennials, which are flowering plants that keep growing over several years.

Use rocks, driftwood, old stuff, sand, gravel — and plants.

Plant short plants in front, tall plants in back.

Time to relax. Get cold drinks or hot chocolates for yourself and your friends while you sit back and look over all you've done. Pretty cool, huh? Now you can finally enjoy what you have . . . until other ideas emerge.

A PANEL-METHOD PLAYHOUSE

Carolyn Miller devised this "knock-down" playhouse with sections that can be easily moved or stored in the winter. She used lightweight yet durable materials and showed that there are no limits to the decorating possibilities. Since very young children use this playhouse, she wisely left out any glass in the windows.

> **"** I built this playhouse for my niece, Pearl, using a panel method I designed that allows for easy disassembly and moving. Pearl's house is built with 2×2s and ¼" plywood for the walls, 2×2s and Shakertown shingles for the roof, and 4"-long by ¼"-diameter bolts hold the walls and roof panels together. The floor is framed with 2×4s, and the walls are screwed to the floor with 3"-long lag screws. In the pictures, my grandson, Anthony, is discovering the joys of a playhouse."

— Carolyn Miller

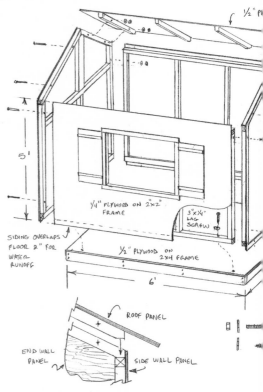

Part 3

THE ADVANCED CLUBHOUSE

BUILDING A BACKYARD HIDEAWAY

This book is a shelter-building journey for grown-ups as well as kids. I encourage everyone, kids and new builders alike, to get a feel for carpentry tools, discover salvage yards, hardware stores, and lumberyards, and then find a site, build a shelter, and finish it inside and out.

So you're older now . . . so what? You can still take the journey and build your own "club-house," be it a studio, office, guesthouse, potting shed, hermitage, hideout, shack, or cabin. In this part of the book, I'll demonstrate how to build an 8-foot by 15-foot permanent structure — an affordable project that *anyone* who can swing a hammer can build with his or her own hands. Once you see how it all goes together, you can use this design, change the measurements to suit your needs, or build something altogether different.

Many of the building methods used for the Classic Clubhouse described in part 2 are the same ones you'll use to build this larger shelter.

If you feel overwhelmed, build the Classic Clubhouse first, give it to the kids, then tackle your own project.

At only 120 square feet on the ground, this 8-foot by 15-foot retreat is adaptable to many uses, while the shape allows it to fit in a rela-tively tight space. The roof will be a gable design to allow room for a loft and to give it an elegant look both inside and out. This house is also por-table: The self-bracing plywood construction will support this little house should it be lifted or built onto a flatbed or trailer. With a road height of less than 14 feet, it is low enough to pass under bridges.

CHAPTER 8

PLANNING

Where do you start? You have probably seen a potting shed, guest cottage, studio, or some other hideaway you would love to have. You'd also like to get some exercise, enjoy the outdoors, learn to use tools, and create an extra living space in the process. You have a feeling you can do this, fueled by a growing desire that you must.

So look around in your yard or on your land and imagine the shelter you would like to have there. Then list what you would like to do in it, sketch some floor plans with the items from your list in mind, and dream. This chapter will help you.

Legalities

In most localities, construction of a backyard shelter with a footprint of 120 square feet does not require a building permit. Check with your county, city, or neighborhood owners' association to make sure.

Finding the Best Site and Orientation

Now is a good time to decide on the overall size and orientation of your shelter. When you have determined its size, measure it out on the ground, then lay down boards or a rope to outline it. Imagine where the door will be and how it relates to the site. Put a chair on the ground, sit down, and imagine looking out to the best view, then you'll know where you'll want a large window. Also, if your house is nearby, will your new shelter look appealing or will it be in the way of a view?

A good building site offers adequate room for access around all four sides of your shelter and perhaps room on one side for a patio, deck, or garden. Check out where the sun rises and sets . . . perhaps you'd like morning light in the breakfast nook. If you are building on a hillside, try to orient your structure to minimize digging into the hill, which can bring on erosion problems later.

Designing It

There are many ways you can arrange your shelter. Sleeping, eating, working, and relaxing can all happen in a surprisingly small space. You could start by building a Zen-like empty room and then decide how you'll use it later. Or you may want to figure out every detail beforehand. It's your choice. This is where your dream place becomes something real.

First make a list: Write down what you would like to do in your shelter, then list all the things you would need to accomplish it. For example, if you want to paint landscapes, you'll need space for your easel, supplies, and other equipment; a place to rest or to stand back and evaluate your progress; and good lighting. You might want to look in magazines and design books for art studio ideas.

Also, think about how your shelter will relate to the site you've chosen. Will you want to have a garden outside the door or a small patio or a hot tub for relaxing? Does the space outside the shelter offer good sunlight for a garden or privacy for a hot tub?

Then begin to sketch out your ideas. With your list handy, start with a rectangle (with our 8-foot by 15-foot project size in mind), and label the different areas of the rectangle with "painting area," "storage," "computer/printer," and so on, depending on what you want to do. Next, think about where you want to enter your space and where to let in light and air. What will the inside look like? The outside? When sketching, feel free to add as much space as you'd like, but keep in mind that you are going to do the building.

Once you've established the size of your space and how you'll use it, draw more detailed sketches of your floor plan and side views. If you've never done this before, the exercise can be challenging, but try to get your ideas down as clearly as possible. And ignore negative criticism, be it from your family or friends or even yourself . . . this is your place and you can build it the way you want it!

Our example project will be a hideaway with a loft and room for a studio workspace and/or living quarters. It's the first of the plans on facing page. If it doesn't appeal to you, take a look at the other plans, or sketch out your own.

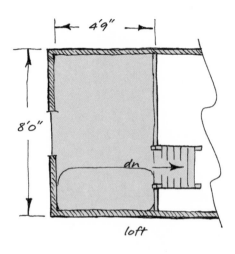

loft

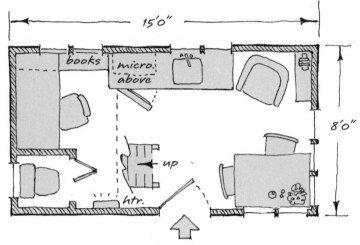

lower level

SAMPLE
HIDEAWAY PLANS

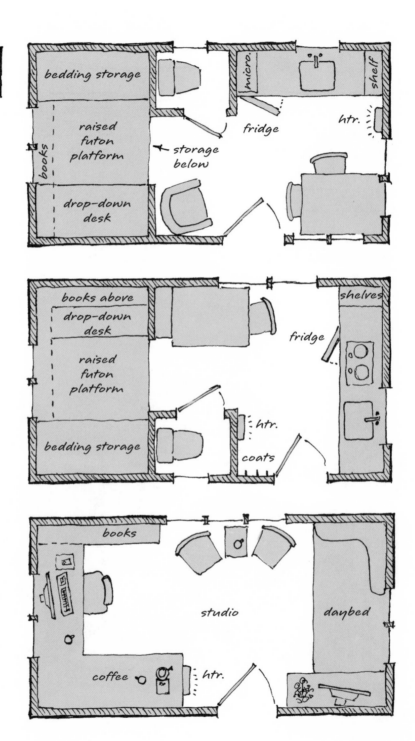

bedding storage

books

raised
futon
platform

drop-down
desk

storage
below

micro.

shelf

fridge

htr.

books above

drop-down
desk

raised
futon
platform

bedding storage

shelves

fridge

htr.

coats

books

studio

daybed

coffee

htr.

Choosing Windows and a Door

Now that you have a good idea of what you want to build, you'll need to think about windows and a door. To determine the size of the wall openings, it is wise to have the windows and door on hand or at least know their exact dimensions.

You can install used windows or new ones, and the ultimate size of them will be up to you and what is available. For such a small space, I believe single-glazed windows are adequate for most climates outside Alaska. Have at least one openable window near each end of your shelter for good cross-ventilation.

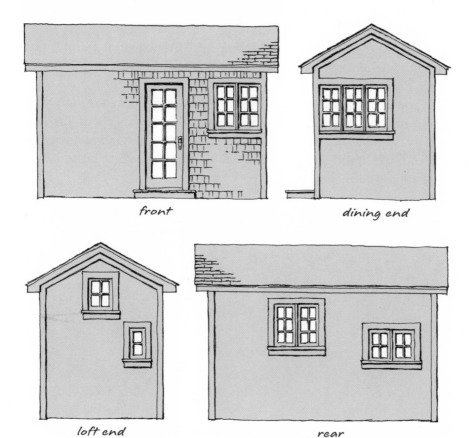

DOOR AND WINDOW LOCATIONS

front

dining end

loft end

rear

A good door for your shelter would be at least 30″ wide, exterior-grade, and already on its hinges in a frame or doorjamb. These "prehung" doors are offered in many styles at home centers and lumberyards. Some recycled building-supply stores sell salvaged prehung doors as well, which might have just the right look and are usually far more economical than new ones.

In this example project, we'll use some recycled windows that are 18″ wide by 36″ tall, and then we'll gang them up to make 36″ by 36″-wide and 36″ by 54″-wide windows. Above the loft, we'll use a 20″ by 25″ barn sash window, which is available in many large home centers. This can be ganged up as well. For the tiny toilet room/closet, we'll use a recycled window that is only 12″ by 24″. The door will be 30″ wide by 80″ tall.

Drawing a Floor Plan

Once you've decided what you want in your space and have determined the window and door sizes, you can finally draw a dimensional floor plan to scale. Yes, this might take you back to high school drafting class, but a simple floor plan with dimensions is relatively easy to produce and quite crucial . . . you'll be glad you did it.

When you have the windows and the door you want, list each one and its dimensions on your floor plan. Put a letter beside each window on the plan, then use the same letter to identify the corresponding window measurements on your list. This list, called a schedule, will tell you how large to build each window and door opening.

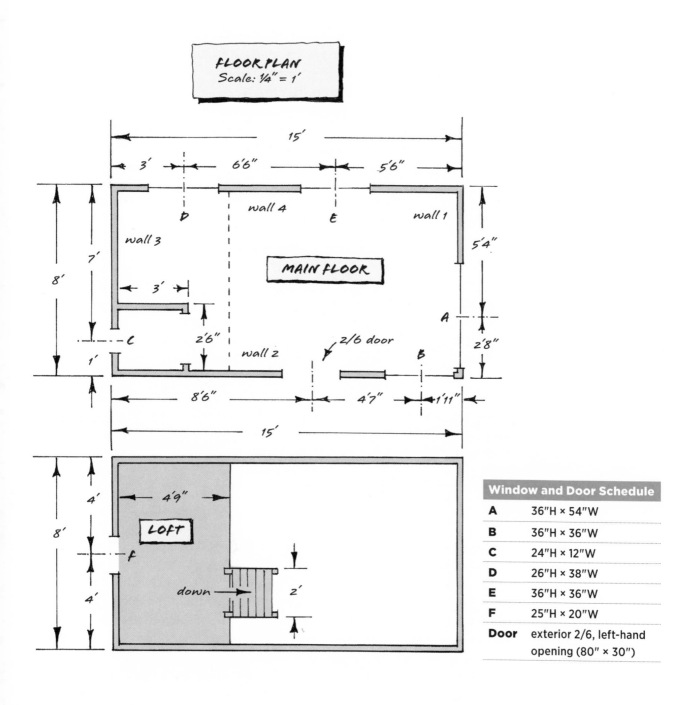

FLOORPLAN
Scale: ¼" = 1'

15'

3'   6'6"   5'6"

wall 4

wall 1

D   E

wall 3

5'4"

7'

8'

MAIN FLOOR

3'

A

2'6"

2'8"

C

wall 2

2/6 door

B

1'

8'6"   4'7"   1'11"

15'

LOFT

4'

4'9"

8'

f

down   2'

4'

Window and Door Schedule	
A	36"H × 54"W
B	36"H × 36"W
C	24"H × 12"W
D	26"H × 38"W
E	36"H × 36"W
F	25"H × 20"W
Door	exterior 2/6, left-hand opening (80" × 30")

One way to draw your plan is to use graph paper, and decide how many inches each little square will be (the scale). Another way is to get an architect's scale at any drafting or office-supply store. With this three-sided ruler, you can choose a scale for your plan. With "scale," you are saying that ¼″, ½″, or some other measurement on your paper equals 1 foot in reality. I like to use the ¼″ scale, but the ½″ scale might be easier to work with for starters. To use this scale, look for the ½ number at the end of the architect's scale. You'll see that the feet begin at 0 and run the length of the ruler. The inches are the tiny marks that begin on the other side of the 0. This way, you can measure out the feet and then add the inches, all from the 0 mark (see the drawing below).

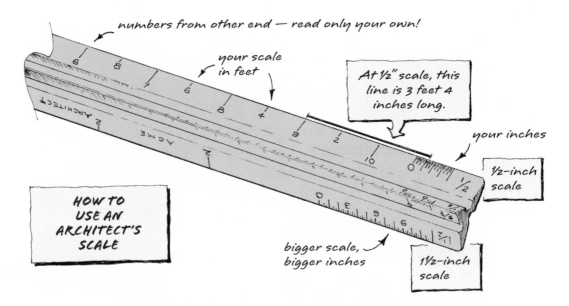

numbers from other end — read only your own!

your scale in feet

At ½″ scale, this line is 3 feet 4 inches long.

your inches

½-inch scale

HOW TO USE AN ARCHITECT'S SCALE

bigger scale, bigger inches

1½-inch scale

To draw your floor plan, get a plastic drafting triangle, a T-square, tape, drawing paper, and a sharp pencil, along with your architect's scale. Find a table with a straight side for your T-square. Tape down a sheet of paper. From your sketch, measure out the length and width of the floor, then draw the walls, as shown on page 143. Look at your rough sketch to locate where you want your window and door openings on the plan. Then with your scale, find the *centers* of the openings on your plan, and measure out to their edges, depending on how wide they are. This plan, along with your outside wall sketches, will provide enough information for you to start your building. Make a copy to take out to your site.

CAD

If you are familiar with computer-aided design (CAD), a scaled floor plan might be easier for you to produce on a CAD program. I still use the simple (some say primitive) lines-on-paper method, which I believe is more efficient for a small-scale project. It's your choice.

Gathering Materials

Now you are ready to get the lumber and other supplies to build your shelter. Each chapter that follows includes a materials list for a specific phase of your project. Of course, you can gather everything at once, but if your supplier is nearby, you might want to get small loads as you build.

In general, it's not difficult to estimate materials. In most cases, you can simply count up the pieces you need, depending on the area of your floor, roof, and walls. It is wise to add a few more pieces to your total, as a cushion; there's always that extra board or two you never thought of in the plans. To estimate wall studs that are set at 16″ on center, calculate one stud per running foot of wall to figure in blocking and built-up corners. To estimate roofing, which is sold by the square foot, find out how many square feet you need to cover, then add 10 percent.

When considering new or used materials, I recommend a balance between ease of construction and low cost. With this in mind, get new materials for the framing, sheathing, and roofing of your shelter. You might find just the right used windows, but if not, try to find barn sash windows, which are inexpensive, scaled nicely, and look good. Of course, higher-priced standard sash and casement windows of all sizes are available, but try to scale your windows to the size of your structure.

Okay, now it's time to begin.

THE ONE THAT (ALMOST) GOT AWAY

Several years ago an old country estate in New Jersey was slated for demolition to make room for a condominium development. Just before the buildings were razed, neighbor John P. Rickerhauser was out walking (fortunately with his camera handy) and spotted this wonderful but neglected playhouse on the grounds. These estate playhouses often had running water, wood- or coal-fired cookstoves, and electric lights, and I suspect this one had it all. The fence alone is an architectural treasure.

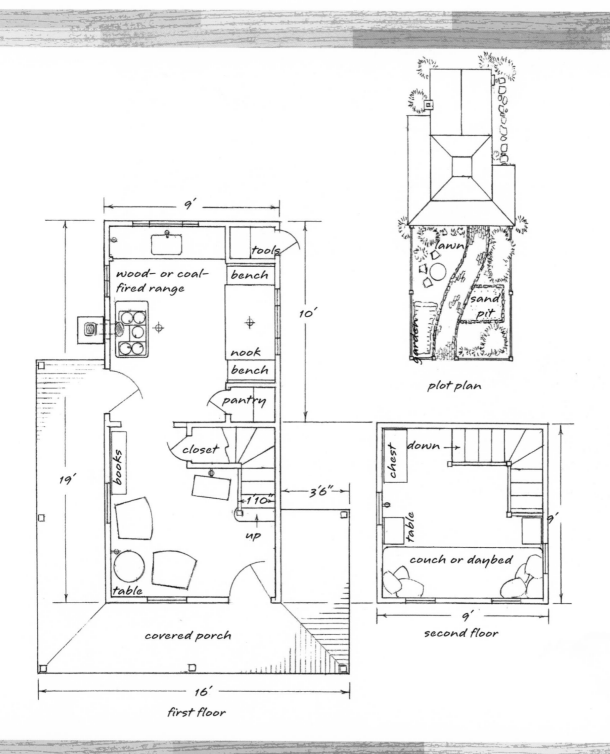

9'

tools

wood- or coal-
fired range

bench

10'

nook
bench

pantry

closet

books

19'

3'6"

1'10"

up

table

covered porch

16'

first floor

plot plan

lawn

garden

sand
pit

down

chest

table

couch or daybed

9'

9'

second floor

CHAPTER 9

BUILDING THE FOUNDATION, SILLS, AND FLOOR

You've found a suitable building site, checked with your city (if necessary), and drawn up your plan. Besides the materials listed below, you'll need the tools listed in chapter 1. You'll need a good set of tall sawhorses. You can also build your own sawhorses, as described in chapter 1, but add 6" to 8" to the length of the legs. You'll also find a shovel and a wheelbarrow helpful for digging, hauling gravel, and mixing concrete (optional).

Foundation and Flooring Materials

Part	Quantity	Description
Foundation base	12	⅔-cubic-foot bags ½" to ¾" crushed rock; *or* gravel (8 cubic feet total); *or*
	12	similar-size bags dry premix concrete
Temporary layout stakes	4	of any size
Foundation blocks	6	concrete pier blocks (see the drawing below)
Foundation sills	2	4×6s, 16 feet long, pressure-treated
Rim joists	2	2×6s, 16 feet long
Floor joists	14	2×6s, 8 feet long
Posts	1 or 2	4×4s, 8 feet long, pressure-treated (optional; you'll need these if the ground is sloped)
Permanent bracing	2 or 3	1×6s, 8 feet long, pressure-treated (optional; you'll need these if the ground is sloped)
Batter board stakes	12	cut from 2×4s, each stake from 2 to 4 feet long
Batter boards and temporary bracing	6	1×3 or 1×4 furring strips, 8 feet long
Floorboards	4	4 × 8-foot sheets ¾"-thick tongue-and-groove OSB or plywood
Adhesive	4	tubes construction adhesive
Nails	5 pounds of each	16d coated sinkers; 8d coated sinkers
Nails	2 pounds	6d coated sinkers
Nails	1 pound	6d or 8d duplex nails

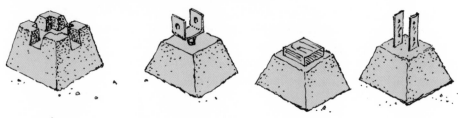

COMMON TYPES OF PIER BLOCK

okay　　　*better*　　　*okay*　　　*better*

Building the Foundation

The foundation will consist of six concrete pier blocks set on gravel or concrete footings.

SET THE STAKES

Step 1. To lay out the foundation approximately, get your tape measure, four temporary stakes, and a hammer. Drive in a stake at each of the corners of an 8-foot by 15-foot rectangle.

Step 2. Have a friend help you measure the diagonals (from corner to corner), adjusting the stakes as needed until the diagonal measurements are equal. If the ground is level, the diagonals should come out to 17 feet (204"). At this point, the measurement doesn't have to be exact; it can be off by an inch or so.

Step 3. Double-check to be sure the stakes are where you want the corners of your building to be.

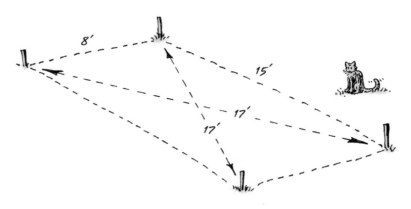

PUT UP BATTER BOARDS

Although these stakes give you an approximate location for your corners, you'll want to find the exact location by using batter boards and string. Batter boards are temporary L-shaped contraptions that help you find the exact corners of your foundation. The following steps may seem fussy, but if your foundation is crooked, your whole project will be thrown off. So get a friend to help, and you'll have this done in no time.

Step 1. Make or buy twelve 2×4 stakes about 2 feet to 4 feet long, depending on whether your site is sloped. Cut eight batter boards, each about 3 feet long, from the 1×3 furring strips.

Step 2. Measure about 2 feet out from each temporary stake, and pound in three 2×4 stakes in an L formation that encloses the small stake. If your site appears to slope, drive shorter stakes at the uppermost corner and longer ones at the lower corners.

Step 3. Nail two batter boards to the 2×4 stakes in the highest corner of the foundation. Use 6d or 8d duplex nails. The batter boards should form an L shape and should be level.

Step 4. The batter boards at all the other corners must be level with the batter boards at this first corner. Attach a string to the top of the first batter board, then pull the string to the next corner, aligning it over the temporary stakes. Have a friend hook a line level to the middle of the string. As your friend watches the level, move the string up or down between the 2×4 stakes, keeping it aligned over the temporary stake. When the string is level, set a 1×3 batter board in place under the string. Have a friend mark the location of its edges on the 2×4 stakes. Then nail it into place, again using duplex nails.

Step 5. Complete the L formation at this second corner by setting and nailing a second batter board level to the first.

Step 6. Repeat this procedure to install the batter boards in the remaining two corners of your foundation. Be patient, and remember that this is only a "rough leveling" — it can be off by an inch or two and still work!

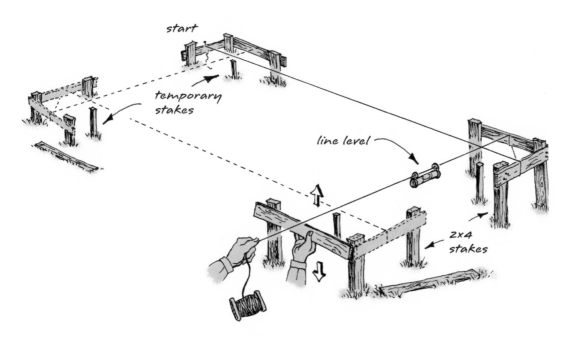

start

temporary stakes

line level

2x4 stakes

SQUARE AND MARK THE STRING

Now that the batter boards are up, you'll need to adjust the string and find the true corners of your foundation.

Step 1. Measure your foundation dimensions at the points where the strings cross in each corner. Have your friend hold the tape hook as steady as possible, at one corner, while you pull it to the next.

Step 2. Move the strings by sliding them along the batter boards, and check again with the tape, until the foundation rectangle is exactly 8 feet wide by 15 feet long and the diagonals in both directions are 17 feet. This can be a bit tricky, but don't pull your hair out — you'll get it eventually, unless the batter boards aren't level.

Step 3. Once the strings are set, clearly mark each point where the string meets the batter boards, just in case someone trips over the string later. A pencil mark will work, or use a nail to hold the string in place. With the corners squared and marked, now you can remove the temporary stakes.

Step 4. Mark the location of the two center piers at the midpoint of the long sides (7½ feet from each corner).

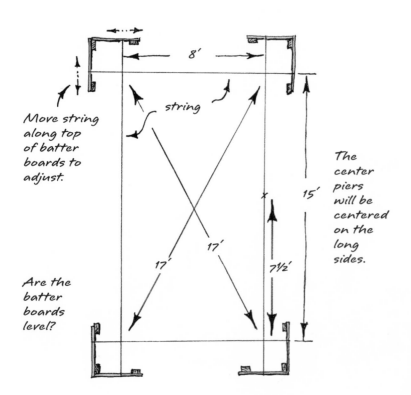

Move string along top of batter boards to adjust.

string

Are the batter boards level?

8'

17'

17'

7½'

15'

The center piers will be centered on the long sides.

High Winds, Earthquakes, and Concrete Footings

If your shelter is exposed to high winds, or you live in earthquake country, you'll want to hold down the structure as securely as possible. Using pier blocks set with embedded steel ties in concrete footings will help. Use three ½-cubic-foot or ⅔-cubic-foot bags of premixed concrete per pier block footing. Dump one or more bags of concrete mix into a clean wheelbarrow, then add water according to the instructions on the bag. Mix with a shovel or a garden hoe. Fill each hole with concrete, then immediately set the pier block as described on facing page. When you are done for the day, remember to thoroughly hose off the wheelbarrow and tools.

SET THE PIER BLOCKS

You will set six pier blocks on gravel, or concrete if you wish (see the box on facing page), using your string to get them in the right place. The point where the strings intersect is the exact corner of the building, which is also the outer corner of the post pocket in each corner pier block (see the drawing below). With this in mind, the footing holes are centered slightly inside the string corners. Here's how to set the blocks:

Step 1. At each corner, measure out a 16″ square on the ground, centered about 2″ inside the corner of the string. The two side holes are centered at the 7½-foot mark and about 2″ inside the string.

Step 2. Using a spade, dig each square hole out to 8″ deep, then fill it to the top with gravel (or concrete).

Step 3. As you set a pier block, have a friend lower a plumb bob from the string corner to the pier block, while you jiggle the block into place, firmly setting it into the packed gravel, as shown below. Level the pier block using your 9″ level.

Step 4. For the side pier blocks, set the edge of the block's post pocket directly under the plumb bob and at the 7½-foot mark.

Step 5. Repeat for all the piers. Leave the string in place.

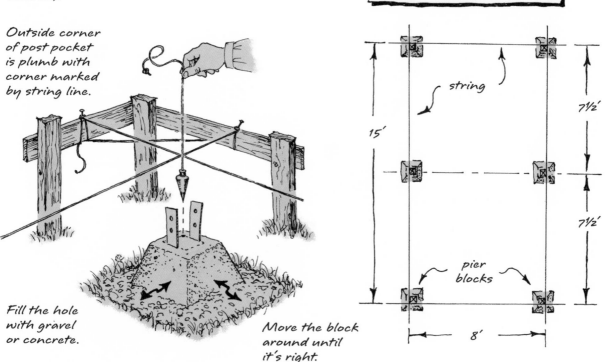

Outside corner of post pocket is plumb with corner marked by string line.

Fill the hole with gravel or concrete.

Move the block around until it's right.

PIER BLOCK LAYOUT

string

pier blocks

15′

7½′

7½′

8′

Making the Sills

Your floor will be supported by two 4×6 beams, or sills. If the ground is uneven or sloping, you may need to add posts to support the sills.

SET THE SILLS

Step 1. Measure and cut two pressure-treated 4×6 sills to exactly 15 feet long. This is a big cut, so draw your cut mark all the way around the sills. If you're hand-sawing, watch the cut lines on the sides as well as the top for a square cut. With a power saw, cut across the top cut mark, then rotate the sill 90°, saw on through, then rotate it and saw again. You'll get a clean cut this way.

Step 2. Set one sill on the highest pier block, and have a friend move it up and down at the other end while you eyeball your level. When it's level, measure the distance from the underside of the sill to the top of the lower pier blocks. If this distance is only a couple of inches, you can settle the highest pier block lower into the gravel until the sill is resting level on the next pier block. If the distance is 2″ or more, you'll need to support the sill with posts at the lower pier blocks. Just cut a post to length out of cedar, redwood, or pressure-treated 4×4 (or from the 4×6 scraps you just cut off).

Step 3. Check for level at the middle pier block in the same way, and cut a post to length if necessary.

Step 4. To level the opposite sill, use an 8-foot-long straight board with a level strapped to it as a homemade long level. While your friend holds the level, measure the distance from the top of each pier block to the bottom edge of the level. Account for the height of the sill. If the remaining distance is greater than 2″, cut a post to size.

If it's less than 2″, you can probably level the pier block simply by shifting it in the gravel base, as long as the gravel remains firmly packed under the pier block.

Step 5. With your friend's help, set up and secure the sills to the pier blocks as necessary. Toenail them to the posts with 8d galvanized box nails. If the sills want to lean or fall over, brace them with temporary stakes, as shown below. Don't take the strings down yet.

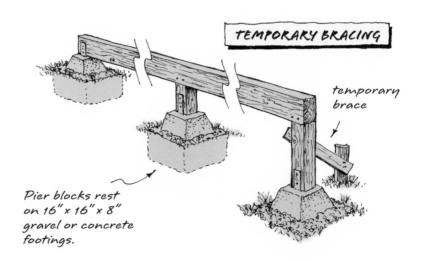

TEMPORARY BRACING

temporary brace

Pier blocks rest on 16″ x 16″ x 8″ gravel or concrete footings.

Step 6. If any of the posts are more than 18" tall, brace them to your beams, with permanent brace boards (see the drawing on page 157). For brace boards, use redwood, cedar, or pressure-treated 1×4s or, better yet, 1×6s. Nail the braces in place with several 8d galvanized box nails at each end.

As you nail them, check the sills to make sure they are in line with your strings. Leave any temporary braces in place for now.

Step 7. When your sills are braced, remove the strings and batter boards . . . finally!

LEVELING THE OPPOSITE SILL

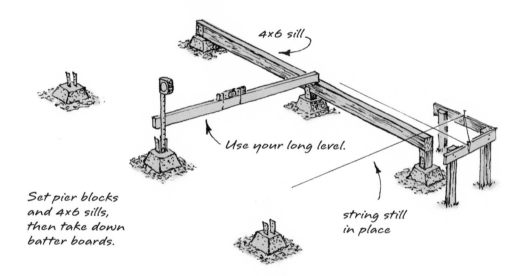

4x6 sill

Use your long level.

Set pier blocks and 4x6 sills, then take down batter boards.

string still in place

Constructing the Floor

Your hideaway will have a floor made of 2×6 joists covered with sheets of tongue-and-groove OSB flooring.

INSTALL THE JOISTS

Step 1. Cut two long 2×6s to 15 feet (180″) long; these will be the rim joists.

Step 2. Lay the two rim joists on edge, side by side on your sawhorses. With your tape measure, make centerline marks every 16″ along the top edge of both boards.

Step 3. Measure to the left of each centerline, and make edge marks on both boards. Using your square, draw edge lines (marking the edge of a joist) across both boards, on both the edge and the flat side. Mark an X next to each edge line, and over the centerline, to show which side of the edge marks the joists will meet (see the drawing at right). For added strength, you'll double the joists at the ends, so mark 2 Xs at each end of the joist.

Step 4. Set one rim joist on edge on the outer edge of a 4×6 sill (see the drawing at right), and toenail it to the sill. The Xs you drew on the board should face inside the foundation.

Step 5. Cut fourteen 2×6 joists to 7 feet 9 inches (93″) long, and place them on the sills at the Xs. Sight along the edge of each joist with your eye. If it's bent or bowed, turn it so it bends up in the middle. The joists should end 1½″ from the outer edge of the other sill.

Step 6. Have a friend hold down each floor joist while you nail the rim joist into it with three 16d nails. A framing hammer (see the box on facing page) is useful here.

Step 7. Set up the opposite rim joist, and check to see that your marks line up the same way.

Step 8. Nail the rim joist to the ends of all the floor joists, and toenail it into the sill. The joists should fit on the sills as shown on facing page.

Step 9. Add more permanent braces from the joists to the posts, if necessary, then remove any temporary braces.

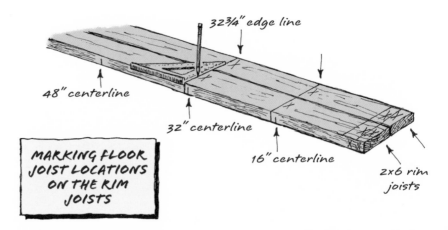

32¾″ edge line
48″ centerline
32″ centerline
16″ centerline
2x6 rim joists

MARKING FLOOR JOIST LOCATIONS ON THE RIM JOISTS

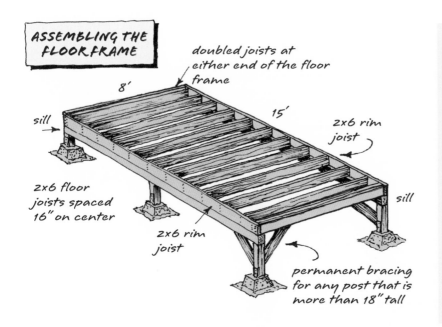

ASSEMBLING THE FLOOR FRAME

doubled joists at either end of the floor frame

8'

sill

2x6 rim joist

15'

2x6 floor joists spaced 16" on center

2x6 rim joist

sill

permanent bracing for any post that is more than 18" tall

Heavier Hammering

For framing, I recommend a 22-ounce framing hammer with a smooth (not "waffle") head. Once you've set a 16d nail, hold the hammer handle well away from the head, and use your whole arm to drive in the nail. With fewer hammer strokes, the nail will have less of a chance to bend, and you will last longer. Keep practicing this to get the feel of your hammer.

NAIL DOWN THE FLOOR

Now that all the joists are nailed together, the next step is to nail down the floor itself. I recommend ⅝"- or ¾"-thick tongue-and-groove OSB in 4-foot by 8-foot sheets. It's inexpensive and strong. Stagger the sheets for extra strength (see the drawing on page 158).

Step 1. Lay out a full sheet of OSB on your joists, line it up neatly to a corner, then lay another to the end of the floor. The two sheets should join over a joist. Using 8d nails, tack the sheets down so they won't be pushed out of place when you begin laying the next row of flooring.

Step 2. You'll want the seams in the flooring to be staggered, so begin the next row of flooring with a 48"-long sheet. If the tongue-and-groove

don't join easily, set a 2×4 block against the edge and pound the two together with a hammer.

Step 3. Cut the sheet to size on sawhorses or on the floor. Set your circular saw blade to cut 1" deep or ¼" below your floor panel. Then use a scrap board under your cut to avoid sawing into the floor.

Step 4. Continue laying and tacking down OSB, staggering the seams, until your floor is covered.

Step 5. Saw off any overhanging scraps while the sheets are in place, so that the panels are now all tacked down and lined up evenly with the outer edge of the floor framing. See how nicely the panels line up to your square corners? This is where foundation fussiness begins to pay off.

continued on next page

Step 6. Nail down all the flooring with 8d coated sinkers or galvanized box nails. Use your regular (not framing) hammer for this. Use one nail every 6″ on the edges and one every 12″ on every inside joist. (To guide your nailing into the inside joists, you can mark the location of the joists right on the panels.)

Flooring Adhesive

Many builders use a construction adhesive such as Liquid Nails on top of the floor joists just before nailing down the flooring, which prevents squeaking from any loose nails and makes a stronger floor. To use adhesive, set a tube in your caulking gun, cut off the tip with a utility knife, and poke a hole through the inside seal. Pump the trigger a few times, then squeeze it gently to squirt out a single line of adhesive on the joists. The adhesive dries quickly, so apply it under one panel at a time.

NAILING DOWN THE FLOOR PANELS

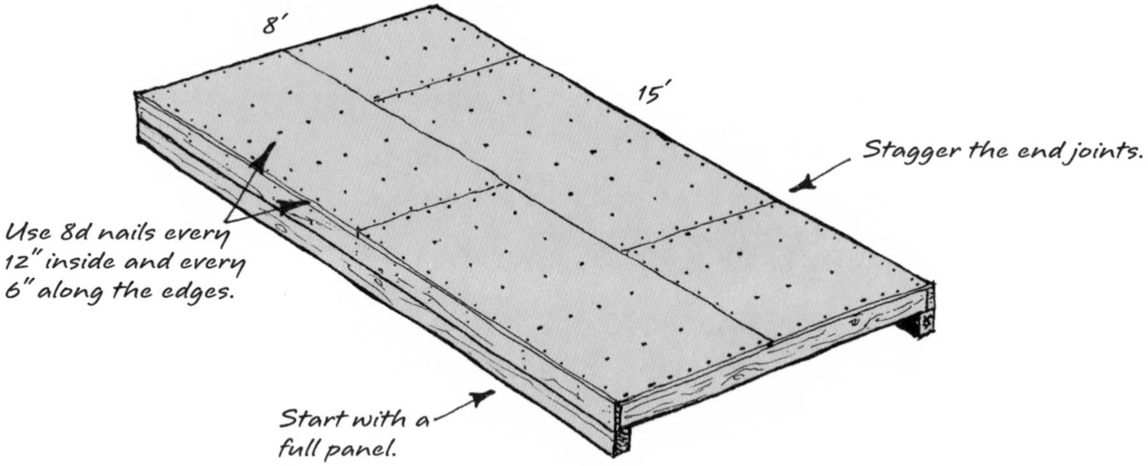

8′

15′

Stagger the end joints.

Use 8d nails every 12″ inside and every 6″ along the edges.

Start with a full panel.

All right — now you can dance on your new floor!

CHAPTER 10

BUILDING THE WALLS

With the framing of the walls, we enter the world of modern house carpentry. I'll show you the way builders lay out and assemble the pieces of wood to make the walls. There is some carpenter language here, but this method of framing will make efficient use of your materials and also get your structure approved should you need a building permit.

You'll frame the walls with 2×4 studs centered every 16″. To save a lot of cutting of 2×4s, I recommend buying the 92⅝″-long precut studs. These will make a framed wall a little more than 8 feet tall — the standard wall height in house construction. Set aside leftover 2×4s and sheathing for the gable-end walls, which you will construct after the roof is on.

Wall Materials

Part	Quantity	Description
Plates	10	2×4s, 8 feet long
Plates	6	2×4s, 16 feet long
Wall studs	60	2×4s, precut to 92⅝" long
Headers	3	4×4s, 8 feet long
Bracing and trim boards	8	1×4s, 12 feet long
Sheathing	14	4 × 8-foot sheets $\frac{7}{16}$"- or ½"-thick CDX plywood *or* OSB
Nails	5 pounds of each	16d coated sinkers; 6d, 7d; *or* 8d coated sinkers

Cutting and Marking the Top and Bottom Plates

To begin building walls, you'll cut and mark the top and bottom plates. From the plan you drew, you'll transfer the locations and dimensions of your door and windows directly to the plates. The marks will then tell you exactly where to nail on the studs (at the Xs), the trimmers (at the Ts), and the cripples (at the Cs).

CUT THE PLATES

Step 1. Set up your sawhorses, and place four 16-foot-long 2×4s on them. Cut all four to 14 feet 5 inches (173″) long. These will be the top and bottom plates for your longer side walls.

Step 2. Set aside four 8-foot-long 2×4s. These will be the top and bottom plates for your shorter end walls.

Step 3. Mark each pair of plates with a big 1, 2, 3, or 4 for each wall number you will build. Set aside the extra plate of each pair. Number the walls on your plan in the same order.

Step 4. Set one plate on the floor for each wall, as shown in the drawing on facing page. Tack them down with a duplex nail or two if they won't stay put.

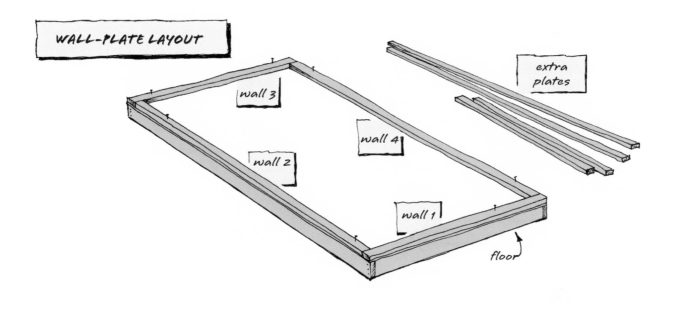

WALL-PLATE LAYOUT

wall 3

wall 4

wall 2

wall 1

floor

extra plates

MARK THE PLATES

Now let's mark the plates where there will be a door, windows, or studs.

Step 1. Spread out your floor plan, with dimensions, on your new floor. Using your plan, measure from the *corner* of the building to the *centers* of your window and door locations, and mark them on the plates. Some builders write CL on these marks to distinguish them from stud centerlines.

Step 2. From the window and door centerlines, measure to the edges of each door and window opening. Look at the plan to see how wide the opening is, then measure half that width to the edges. With your square, draw the edge

lines on the plate. Next to each edge line and away from the center of the opening, write a T, where a trimmer will go.

Step 3. Measure 1½" farther from the center of the opening, draw another edge line, and write an X on the other side of that edge line to mark where a stud will go. So now you have a line, a T, a line, and then an X, as shown in the drawing on page 162.

Step 4. Measure the distance between your trimmer edge lines

to check if that is the actual width of your window opening.

Step 5. For the studs, hook your tape measure to the corner of the building, and mark a centerline every 16" on the plate. Continue to the far end.

continued on next page

Step 6. Make edge marks ¾" past the centerlines, as you did for the floor joists, then draw Xs over the centerline marks. Where a stud falls within a window or door opening, draw a C for cripple, which is a short 2×4 placed above or below a window (see the drawing on page 165). If a window edge is close to a stud, nudge the window opening over to meet the stud to save some lumber, *if* moving the window won't mess up your plan. Check your plan, then redraw your window edge marks carefully. Don't move the studs or cripples, or you'll have problems later.

Step 7. At each end of the plate, draw an X. Where two plates come together at a corner, draw an X at the end of one of them, and three edge lines and Xs on the other one, for what builders call a built-up corner (see the drawing below).

Step 8. Move on and mark all the plates. It will make more sense, and get easier, as you proceed.

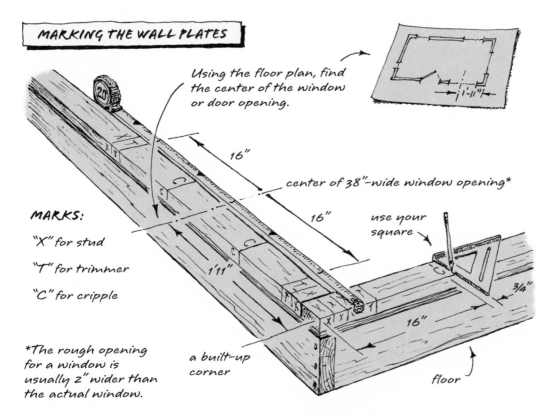

MARKING THE WALL PLATES

Using the floor plan, find the center of the window or door opening.

1'-11"

16"

center of 38"-wide window opening*

16"

use your square

3/4"

16"

MARKS:

"X" for stud

"T" for trimmer

"C" for cripple

1'11"

*The rough opening for a window is usually 2" wider than the actual window.

a built-up corner

floor

Step 9. Once all the plates are marked and the window and door openings are the right size, get the second plates that you had set aside. Lay them flat and edge to edge with the plates you just marked. With your pencil and square, transfer all the marks to these blank plates. Clear all the plates off the floor except for those for wall 1. Now you are ready to cut the pieces and assemble the wall frames.

Building Wall 1

If you are still not sure about all those marks you just drew on the plates, keep going and things will become clearer. Beginning with wall 1, you'll assemble each wall on the floor, using your plan and the marks on the plates. The large window opening in wall 1 will be 56″ wide and 38″ tall, and the bottom of it will be 44″ from the floor. With this information, you can figure out the lengths of all the pieces and then assemble the wall, starting with the studs.

ASSEMBLE THE STUDS AND PLATES

Step 1. On your floor, arrange the top and bottom plates on edge and about 8 feet apart for wall 1. The plate nearest the edge of the floor where this wall will go will be the *bottom* plate.

Step 2. Lay down a 92⅝″ precut 2×4 stud over each X, so the layout begins to look like the drawing on page 165.

Step 3. The ends of this wall are "built up," so we will need to assemble three 2×4 blocks (scraps are okay) inside of two studs, as shown below. Use your square to check that the ends are square, and then drive three 16d nails through the sides of the studs into each block from both sides. Set the built-up ends in place between the plates.

Step 4. To start nailing the wall frame together, set a stud with its edge to the edge line and covering the X, and hold it in place with your foot or knee. With your framing hammer, drive two 16d nails through the plate into the stud. For the built-up ends, nail two nails into each stud and into the block.

Step 5. Continue until all the studs are nailed to the plate.

Step 6. Move to the other plate, and nail it to all the studs as well.

Nailing Tips

Wall frames are usually nailed on the floor, with pieces laid on edge. To start, step on the stud and set the nail into the plate. Then, with your foot on the stud, nail through the plate and into the stud, swinging with your whole arm. When the nail is through the plate, check to see that the pieces are flush and the stud/cripple/trimmer is lined up where it should be. Finish nailing it in. This takes a little practice, so be patient.

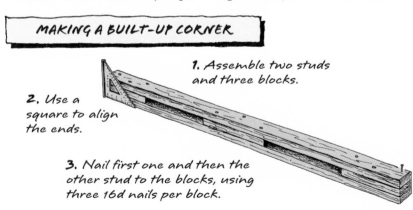

MAKING A BUILT-UP CORNER

1. Assemble two studs and three blocks.

2. Use a square to align the ends.

3. Nail first one and then the other stud to the blocks, using three 16d nails per block.

FRAME THE WINDOW

Next, you'll add the pieces that frame the window. These are called the trimmers, window rough sills, window headers, and cripples.

Step 1. Go to the studs set next to the T marks on the plates. From the bottom of these studs, measure to 41″ and then 82″, and at each location draw edge lines with your pencil and square. *Above* the 41″ edge line, write an S for sill; *above* the 82″ edge line, write an H for header. You just marked where the rough sill and the header will go for your window.

Step 2. Measure the distance along the bottom plate under the window to get the length of the window rough sill and header. The header should be 59″ long, which is the width of the window plus 3″ for the thickness of the two trimmers.

Step 3. Cut five 2×4s to 41″ long for trimmers and cripples. Set all four into place on the T and the C marks on the bottom plate. Nail the trimmers to the studs with 12d nails, then drive two nails through the bottom plate into each trimmer and cripple end.

Step 4. Cut a 2×4 to 59″ long for a window rough sill. Set the sill in place on the trimmers and cripples. It should line up with the edge line you drew on the studs. Drive two nails through the studs into the sill ends and then two nails through the sill into each trimmer end and cripple end. Use 12d or 16d nails.

Step 5. Cut two 2×4s to 38″ long for the upper trimmers. Set these on the sills, and nail them into the studs with two or three 12d nails.

Step 6. Cut a 4×4 or two 2×4s to 59″ long for your window header. With the 2×4s, make a header sandwich by nailing them together with filler scraps of ½″ plywood or OSB to make the header 3½″ thick.

Step 7. Set the header, with the 2×4 edges on the trimmers. Drive two or three nails through the studs into each end of the header.

Step 8. Cut five short trimmers and cripples that go between the top of the window header and the top plate. Measure the vertical distance, then cut four 2×4 blocks to fit. Drive two 12d nails through the top plate into each block. Toenail the blocks into the top of the header with 6d nails.

Step 9. Check your window opening once more. It should be 38″ high by 56″ long.

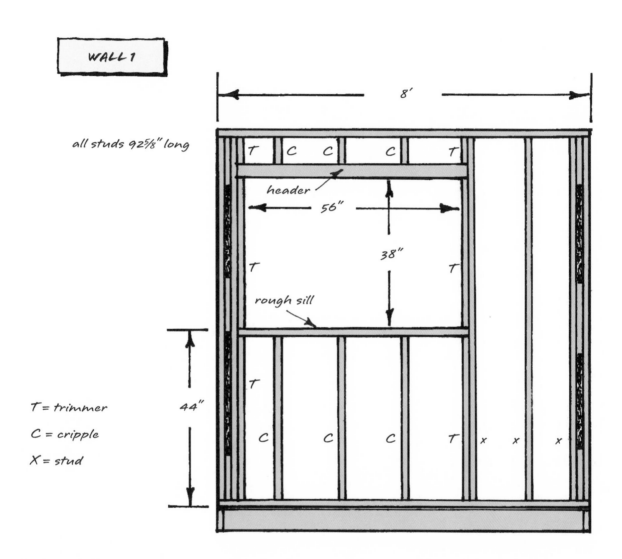

WALL 1

all studs 92⅝" long

8'

T C C C T

header

56"

38"

rough sill

T   T

T

44"

T

C   C   C   T   x   x   x

T = trimmer

C = cripple

X = stud

RAISE WALL 1

Step 1. To raise wall 1, first lift or pry the top plate off the floor enough to slide a 2×4 scrap under it. Then you can grab hold.

Step 2. Have a friend help you lift the wall and nudge it to the edge of the floor. Plumb and brace the wall in place.

Step 3. Nail the bottom plate into the floor between each stud, using 16d nails.

Building Wall 2

Frame the door on wall 2 with the following in mind. Assuming you have a prehung door that is 30" wide by 80" tall, you'll need to add 2½" to the height of the door opening to include the threshold and 2" to the width to include the doorjamb and some wiggle room. Therefore, your door rough opening needs to be 82½" high and 32" wide. Since the bottom plate is 1½" thick, the trimmers will be 81" long. The header will then be 35" long to include the thickness of the two trimmers.

RAISE WALL 2

The longer wall frames are heavy, so once you have nailed wall 2 together, have a friend or two help you raise it.

Step 1. Lay the plates for wall 2 on the floor. Then cut the pieces and assemble wall 2 in the same way as you did for wall 1.

Step 2. Lift or pry the top plate off the floor enough to slide a 2×4 scrap under it. With one or two people helping, lift the wall, nudge it to the edge of the floor, and set it snugly against wall 1.

Step 3. Tack a single 16d nail through the end stud of wall 2 into wall 1, then plumb and brace wall 2 as you did wall 1.

Step 4. Nail the bottom plate into the floor between each stud *except* in the door opening. Use 16d nails.

Step 5. Nail through the end stud of wall 2 firmly into the studs and blocks of the built-up corner of wall 1, using five or six 16d nails.

Step 6. Saw off the bottom plate between the doorway trimmers.

Choosing a Door

Most new doors are sold as prehung units, meaning they are already hung on hinges in a wooden frame or jamb. At the lumberyard, they will call a 30"-wide door a 2/6 door, meaning it is 2 feet 6 inches wide. If you find a really cool unframed door, you can make your own jamb for it and apply the hinges. This is discussed more on page 199. If this is your first door installation, I recommend buying a new prehung unit, which usually comes with its own installation instructions.

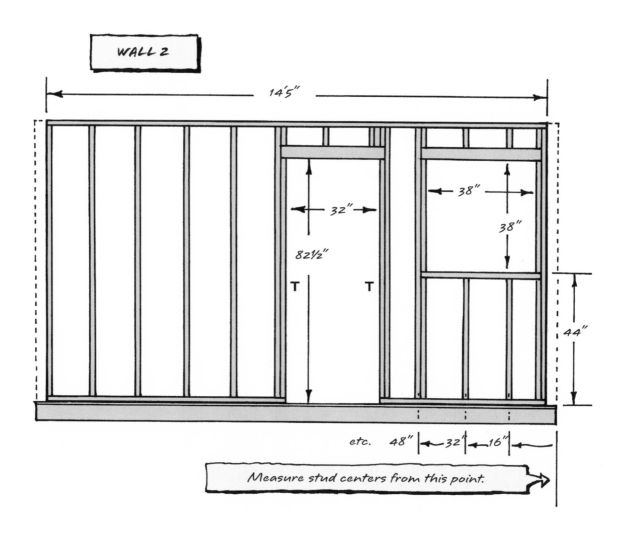

WALL 2

14'5"

32"

82½"

T   T

38"

38"

44"

etc.   48"   32"   16"

Measure stud centers from this point.

Building Wall 3

This wall has two small windows, a low one for the toilet room or closet and a high one that extends above the top plate for the loft. Look at your floor plan to find the window-opening centers and at your side views for the window-opening heights. Cut the pieces and assemble the wall frame, as you did with walls 1 and 2.

When you have marked both plates, take the top plate to your sawhorses and cut out the piece to allow for the frame for the loft window. The 35½" edge lines will be your cut marks. Then bring the pieces back to the floor to assemble the wall.

When wall 3 is framed, lift it up, tack it to wall 2, plumb and brace it, and then nail it to the foor. Then, with five or six 16d nails, attach it to wall 2.

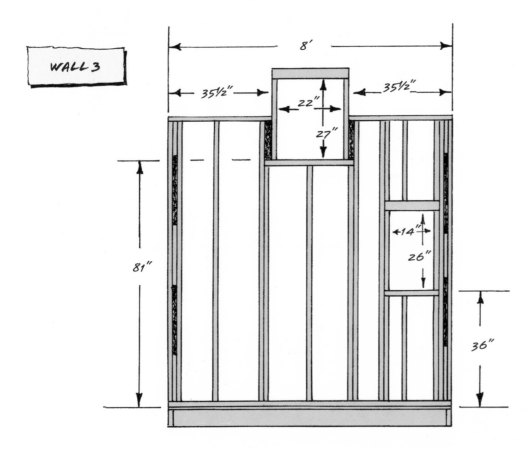

Building Wall 4

This wall has a low under-loft window as well as a higher window for the kitchen counter. Depending on the size of the windows you've chosen, mark and cut the pieces and assemble the wall frame, as shown in the wall 4 drawing below. Then lift it into place, tack it to both wall 3 and wall 1, brace it, and nail it first into the floor, and then into the other walls.

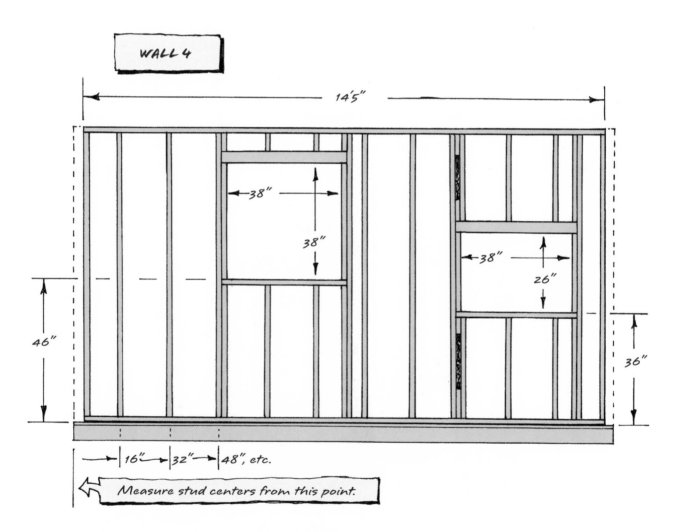

WALL 4

14'5"

38"

38"

38"

26"

46"

36"

16"   32"   48", etc.

Measure stud centers from this point.

Plumb the Walls

As you build the walls, they may get knocked off-plumb by all the pounding and nudging. If so, they will need to be straightened out and then rebraced before you cover the walls with sheathing.

PLUMB AND REBRACE THE WALLS

Step 1. First, check that the tops of all the plates are even at the corners. If they're not, pound down any high places to even them out.

Step 2. Check the wall corners to see if they are still plumb. If they're not, loosen up the braces so you can re-plumb them.

Step 3. Have a friend hold one of the loosened brace boards, ready to nail it in. Have another friend nudge the wall back to plumb, while you hold your long level to an outside corner. When it looks good on both sides, yell, "Hold it!" If it still looks good, then yell, "Nail it in!"

Step 4. Repeat until all the corners are plumb in both directions.

Step 5. If the walls bow in or out at the top, use a cross brace from the top of a stud to the bottom of a stud on the opposing wall, or brace it to a stake in the ground (see the drawing below).

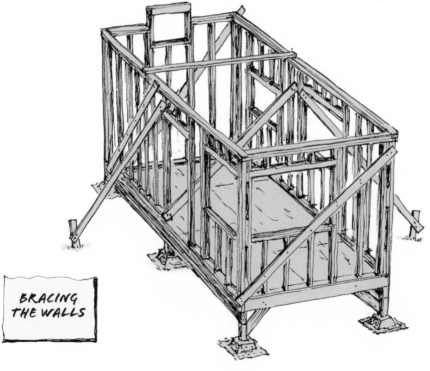

BRACING THE WALLS

Installing the Second Top Plate

This second top plate will tie all the walls together and help straighten them out. We will cut the top-plate boards so they overlap the original top plates at the corners.

ATTACH THE SECOND TOP PLATE

Step 1. Cut two 2×4 pieces 15 feet (180") long and two pieces 7 feet 5 inches (89") long.

Step 2. Set the plates flat on top of your walls. (You might have to loosen a brace or two.) If a wall should happen to bend or bow in, and the top plate also bends a bit, set the top plate so that it bends the opposite way to cancel out the bow in the wall.

Step 3. Nail the top plates onto the top of the original plates with two 12d or 16d nails every 16" to 24". Use three nails at the overlapped corners to tie the walls adequately. If necessary, add a brace board to the floor or across the plates to keep the long walls parallel.

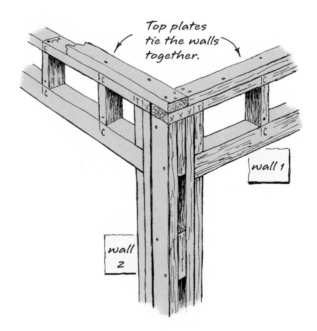

Top plates tie the walls together.

wall 1

wall 2

Covering the Walls

I recommend covering the outside of the walls with ½"-thick CDX plywood or OSB for economy and strength. Either material is strong enough to withstand earthquakes, high winds, or a trip down the highway, should you ever want to move your shelter. OSB is the less expensive material, but plywood accepts shingles or siding a little better. Later, you'll add the exterior siding of your choice (see chapter 7) and interior pine paneling or drywall.

If you laid out your studs at 16" centers, then you should be able to nail up your panels edge to edge without any trimming.

Setting Up a Panel Rest

There's a trick to getting the most out of 8-foot-long sheathing panels: Get a long, straight 1×4 or 2×4 and nail it to the outer floor joist or rim joist to make a ledge, or rest, for the panels. The top of the rest, should be about 5¼" above the bottom of the floor joist, or high enough so the panel covers at least the lower half of the top plate. This way, the panel will reach both the lower and upper plates to help brace your framing (see the drawing at right). Later, after you install the panels, you can cover the remainder of the joist with sheathing scraps. The roof and a soffit board will cover any gap left at the very top.

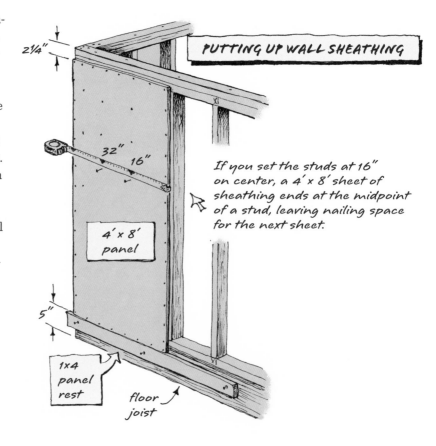

PUTTING UP WALL SHEATHING

2¼"

32"   16"

4' x 8' panel

5"

1x4 panel rest

floor joist

If you set the studs at 16" on center, a 4' x 8' sheet of sheathing ends at the midpoint of a stud, leaving nailing space for the next sheet.

Working with 9-Foot Panels

Plywood and OSB siding are also available in 9-foot-long panels. If you use these, cut them to 8'8" long. Set your panel rest to ½" *below* the bottom of your floor joists and nail the panels in place. The panels should then reach the top of your wall frame. If this is your finished siding and it's exposed to the weather, use galvanized 8d box nails or special siding nails.

MARK AND CUT THE PANELS

Step 1. At the end of a wall, set a panel on the panel rest and have a friend hold the panel to the wall, or tack it to the wall with a couple of nails.

Step 2. Now go inside and use a pencil to trace the edges of any window or door openings onto the panel. These will be your cut lines. Also check to make sure the panel's long vertical edge is centered on a stud so that the next panel will have a nailing surface.

Step 3. Take the panel down and place it on your sawhorses. Cut out the window opening with your circular saw. You may want to set two wide planks on your sawhorses to better support the panel. To avoid deep cuts in the planks, adjust your saw blade so that it cuts only ⅛" deeper than the thickness of the panel. Wear your goggles!

NAIL IN THE PANELS

Step 1. Set the panel back on the rest, and check to see that it fits. For a superstrong bond, apply adhesive such as Liquid Nails on the studs and at the very top and bottom of the panel before nailing.

Step 2. Nail the panel in place with 6d, 7d, or 8d coated sinkers. Drive a nail every 6" all around the edge of the panel and every 12" in the center studs. (To find the center studs, measure across the panel to 16" and 32".) Try to angle some

nails into the floor joist, if possible, since there is not much nailing surface there. Use your lighter-weight hammer for these nails.

Step 3. Once you have finished paneling one wall, remove the braces from the next wall, panel it, and so on. If the rim joist sides are exposed, remember to cover them with scrap pieces of paneling so your building is evenly covered. Unlike the case for siding, cover the joists only to their bottom edge.

Step 4. On the gable-end walls, leave off any paneling above the windows. You can put up these pieces once you complete the upper framing for the gable ends.

Your walls are covered — good work!

KAI AND BRI'S SHINGLE-STYLE COTTAGE

David Lindemulder is a California architect who demonstrates that there are no limits regarding the construction of playhouses. His joyful experience with play sheds in his boyhood Detroit neighborhood might very well have influenced his choice of career and certainly this elegant creation.

" I would guess that most of us who have built playhouses as adults were undoubtedly influenced by our own childhood experience with a playhouse, having had one or wishing we did. Unfortunately, I only wished. There were two playhouses in my Detroit neighborhood that I certainly envied. Both were sheds attached to garages, built for kids but eventually converted to storage. We had a great four years in them before the lawn mowers moved in. In one I remember playing fort and with great joy hooking the door and closing the window shutters so no one could get in. Hotter than hell in the summer but no problem! Even though I had play tents and a rough tree house once, that playhouse was the primary influence on my building one 35 years later for my own kids.

The design of my daughters' playhouse really came from the fertile imagination of my eldest. One winter I asked her to draw what she envisioned the playhouse to look like. My own contemporary notions were soon put aside, as kids see things that would be fun much more clearly. A steeply pitched roof with a tower and a loft were absolutely essential. The ideal site was not out in the open where Dad would have put it but tucked away in an overgrown portion of the yard. Dad had to make this buildable, and of course build it, but who's quibbling?

Even though a year of weekends and evenings went into the construction, it was worth it. This is the sort of thing that most never do, some do once, and a fortunate few get to do several times."

— *David Lindemulder*

CHAPTER 11

BUILDING THE ROOF

You've had a nice rest, right? Now let's take a look at the roof. The Classic Clubhouse of part 2 uses a basic boards-on-beams style of roof, which is fine but limited to a very small structure. The little house you're building here will use a gable roof that is framed cathedral style. This will give the inside a spacious feeling and room for a loft.

About Roof Pitch

A gable roof is built at an angle, or pitch. Pitch is a proportion that tells you how steep a roof is. A standard roof pitch varies from 1:12 to 12:12, and sometimes steeper. The first number is the height of the rise, or the vertical dimension; the second number is the length of the run, or the horizontal dimension. If the pitch is 1:12, then the roof rises 1 foot over a 12-foot run and is nearly flat. If the pitch is 12:12, then the roof rises 12 feet over a 12-foot run and is quite steep.

Roof Materials

Part	Quantity	Description
Ridge and fascia boards	3	2×6s, 18 feet long
Rafters	14	2×6s, 12 feet long; *or*
	28	2×6s, 6 feet long
Collar ties	2	2×6s, 8 feet long
Temporary bracing	6	1×4s, 8 to 12 feet long (you can use the same temporary braces you used on the walls)
Temporary bracing	4	2×4s, 12 feet long (you can use these later for the loft)
Roof trim	2	1×8 pine or cedar boards, 12 feet long (optional; see page 189)
Roof sheathing	7	4 × 8-foot sheets ½"-thick plywood or OSB
Roof underlayment	1 roll	15-pound felt
Drip edge	6	10-foot lengths 1½" × 2⅝" aluminum drip edge (see illustration on page 189)
Shingles	2 squares (200 sq. ft.)	three-tab or similar asphalt shingles
Ridge venting	16 lineal feet	shingle-over style
Soffit venting	1 roll	3-foot-wide × 5-foot-long × ¼"- or ⅛"-mesh galvanized wire hardware cloth
Soffits	4	1×8 pine or cedar boards, 10 feet long
Nails	2 pounds	16d galvanized box nails
Nails	1 pound of each	6d galvanized box nails, for the trim boards; 6d duplex nails, for the brace boards; ¾"- or 1"-long galvanized roofing nails
Nails	5 pounds	6d, 7d, or 8d galvanized box nails

Marking and Cutting the Roof Framing

This gable roof will have a 6:12 pitch, which will shed water nicely but won't be too steep to work on. For convenience, you can reduce this proportion to 1:2. The roof has a span of 8 feet, so half of that, the run of a rafter, is 4 feet. From your 1:2 proportion, you can find the rise, which will be 2 feet.

With this valuable information, you can now determine the length of your rafter. One way is to use the Pythagorean theorem; however, that would require adjustments. Another method is to draw a rafter diagram to scale using drafting tools and an architect's scale. I recommend the 1" scale. This way, you can literally draw out your rafter to its exact shape, then measure its length with your architect's scale.

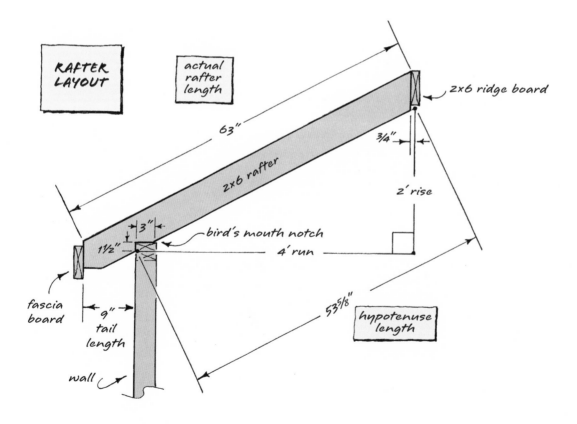

The diagram method will also help you determine the details of your rafters. As you can see in the illustration on facing page, the rafter ends at the ridge board and the thickness of the ridge board will shorten the rafter length. Conversely, the part of the rafter that extends beyond the wall, known as the tail, will lengthen the rafter, depending on how much overhang you want.

You'll cut a notch called a bird's mouth into each rafter so that it will rest solidly on the top plate of the wall. If sheathing covers the wall framing, remember to add its thickness to the width of the bird's mouth.

Now you can measure and cut out a rafter. In this demonstration, the sheathing is *not* covering the wall at the bird's mouth. If there is sheathing, add its thickness to your bird's-mouth cutout.

MARK AND CUT THE TEST RAFTERS

Step 1. To start out, set your rafter square at one end of a 6-foot length of 2×6.

Step 2. Looking at the rows of numbers, or scales, on the square, find the "common" scale, which will you give you the angle cuts for common rafters. Keeping the square snug against the 2×6, tilt the square until the 6 on the common scale lines up with the edge of the 2×6. Mark the angle on the board.

Step 3. Cut off the end, following the angled cut line. Measure 63″ down the board, mark the bottom angle the same way, and cut it.

continued on next page

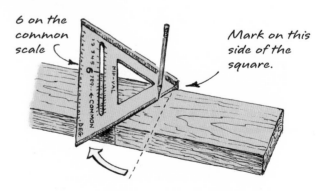

TO FIND THE ANGLE FOR A 6:12-PITCH RAFTER

6 on the common scale

Mark on this side of the square.

Step 4. Cut off the 1½″ by 3″ wedge from the bottom end of the rafter, as shown in the drawing below. Then measure 9″ from the tail for the rafter, and cut out the 1½″ by 3″ bird's-mouth notch, as shown below. Because a circular saw won't cut out the bird's mouth cleanly, use your handsaw to finish the cut.

Step 5. Once you have cut your rafter, use it as a template to make a second test rafter. Simply lay the cut rafter on another 2×6 and carefully redraw the cut lines and cutouts. You'll use these two as a test after you put up the ridge board.

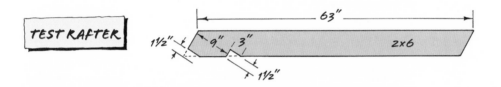

TEST RAFTER

1½″   9″   3″   63″   2×6   1½″

CUT AND MARK THE RIDGE BOARD

At the top of your roof, the ridge board helps line up all the rafters and supports them as well. To make your ridge board:

Step 1. Lay a 2×6 on your sawhorses, and cut it to 17 feet long. This is the length of your building plus 12″ on each end for an overhang.

Step 2. To mark it for the rafters, lay it flat. Measure and draw an edge line 12″ in from one end, which represents the outside edge of your building. Draw an X on the *inside* of this line, which represents the position of the first rafter.

Pound in a small nail at this edge line.

Step 3. Hook your tape measure on the nail, and use it to mark edge lines every 16″. Use your square to draw the lines, then draw Xs on the same side of the edge lines as you drew the first X. At the far end of the ridge board, you can omit the last rafter, leaving a 20″ space.

Step 4. Draw another edge line 12″ in from the far end of your ridge board. Draw an X on the opposite side of this edge line that you drew the rest of the Xs (see the drawing below).

Step 5. Using your square and pencil, transfer all the lines and Xs onto the other side of the ridge board.

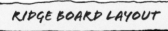

RIDGE BOARD LAYOUT

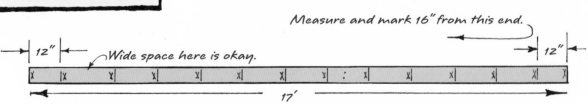

Measure and mark 16″ from this end.

12″   Wide space here is okay.   12″

17′

CUT AND MARK THE FASCIA BOARDS AND TOP PLATES

The fascia boards, which add strength and a finished look to the bottom of the rafters, are next.

Step 1. Cut two fascia boards the same length as the ridge board (17 feet).

Step 2. Lay the two fascia boards and the ridge board flat and side by side. Transfer all the edge lines and Xs from the ridge board to one side of each of the fascia boards, then set the fascia boards aside.

Step 3. Next, use the ridge board to transfer the same rafter marks onto the long-wall plates. With the help of a friend and some stepladders, hoist the ridge board onto the top of one of the long walls. Lay the board beside the long wall plate so the edge marks on the ridge board line up with the ends of the building. Carefully transfer all the lines and Xs from the ridge board to the top of the plate.

Step 4. Move the ridge board directly across to the opposite long wall, and repeat.

Framing the Roof

To begin, it will be necessary to prop up the ridge board to hold it in the right position. You already determined that the rise of the roof is 2 feet, or 24" (see page 178). Theoretically, the bottom of the ridge board should be set at that distance — 2 feet — to meet the ends of the rafters. However, the bird's-mouth notch will *lower* the rafters 1½", so the actual distance from the *top* of the wall plates to the *bottom* of the ridge board becomes: 24" − 1½" = 22½". The next step is to support the ridge board to receive the rafters.

PROP UP THE RIDGE BOARD

Step 1. Find the centers of the short walls, which are 48" in from the outside corners, and mark that spot on the top plate of each short wall.

Step 2. Get two 2×4s that are 8 feet long to use as prop boards, and two blocks or scraps of 2×4 or 1×6 about 1 foot long.

Step 3. Measure from the top end of each prop board to 22½", and draw an edge line. Using duplex nails, nail on the scrap pieces so their bottom edges are at the 22½" mark.

Step 4. Using 16d duplex nails, attach these prop boards to the centers of the end walls, resting the scrap piece on the top plate, as shown on page 182.

continued on next page

Step 5. Get two more 2×4s that are about 12 feet long, two more 2×4 scraps or blocks, and two or three 1×4s that are 6 to 8 feet long.

Step 6. Measure the distance from your floor to the top of the plates, then add 22½" to find the position of the middle support blocks. Measure out that distance on both long 2×4s, draw an edge line, then nail on the scrap pieces with duplex nails.

Step 7. With two stepladders and two friends to help, lift the ridge board to the top of the end-wall props and set it there on edge. While your friends hold each end steady, set the longer props under the ridge board somewhere in the center of the building and tack those in.

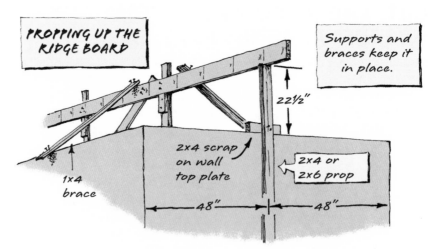

PROPPING UP THE RIDGE BOARD

Supports and braces keep it in place.

22½"

1×4 brace

2x4 scrap on wall top plate

2x4 or 2x6 prop

48"   48"

Step 8. Next, tack two or three 1×4 braces between the top of the ridge board and the top of a long wall, and one more long brace from the side of the ridge board to a short-wall stud near the floor.

Step 9. Sight along the ridge board with your eye. If it is sagging or bowed, adjust the support blocks and 1×4 braces until it is straight. Leave as many of these supports and brace boards in place as is possible until you've installed rafters.

TEST-FIT THE RAFTERS

Now it's time to test-fit the two rafters you've cut.

Step 1. With a friend to help, set the test rafters in place opposite each other, anywhere along the ridge board.

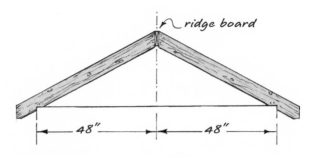

ridge board

48"   48"

Step 2. Check the fit of the rafters. If the bird's mouths fit snugly over the plates, the tops of the rafters meet the top of the ridge board, and the angle cuts fit tightly, great!

Give yourself a big pat on the back and your friend a hug. If they don't fit right, check the measurements and the angles you cut. Trim these rafters or cut new ones, as necessary, until you have a good fit. Be patient; you'll get it right.

CUT THE RAFTERS

When your two test rafters fit, you're ready to cut the rest of the rafters.

Step 1. Write "template" on one of your good test rafters, and use it to mark and cut the remaining 22 rafters the same way, for a total of 24.

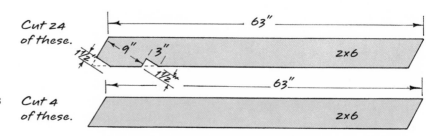

Cut 24 of these.

Cut 4 of these.

Step 2. Cut the four *additional* rafters that will overhang the ends of the roof. Use the same rafter template for these, but don't cut out the bird's mouths or the little wedges at the bottoms. Set these four aside.

BRACE THE WALLS

We will need temporary wall ties to help keep the long walls parallel while you are putting up the rafters. Without them, the long walls will tend to spread out, and they will throw off your rafter fittings. (You can take down these temporary ties once you've installed the permanent collar ties; see page 105.)

Step 1. Cut two 2×4s (or 1×4s) to exactly 8 feet long. These will be the wall ties.

Step 2. Set them flat on top of your long walls, about 4 feet apart near the middle. Align the ends of the ties with the outer edge of the long-wall plates, keeping the ties clear of the Xs that mark the rafter locations. Nail the ties into place with duplex nails.

INSTALL THE RAFTERS

Now it's time to put up all those rafters you cut. First nail in the rafters that attach to the tops of the long walls. You'll install the overhang rafters later, after you've installed the fascia boards. Set the rafters in place one at a time, and roughly in pairs to balance the weight against the ridge board.

Step 1. With a friend holding a rafter in place against the ridge board, toenail it into the wall top plates with 6d, 7d, or 8d nails.

Step 2. Attach the rafter to the ridge board by driving 16d nails through the ridge board into the end of the rafter, toenailing the rafter into the ridge board, or both.

Step 3. Repeat for the rest of the rafters.

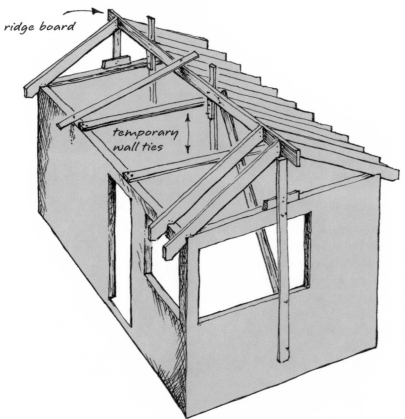

ridge board

temporary wall ties

Note: Rafters are omitted on one side of the building here to show the wall ties. Normally you put up rafters in matching pairs.

INSTALL THE COLLAR TIES

When all the rafters are nailed in, you will need to add permanent braces, called collar ties, to help hold up the roof. These should be installed across rafter pairs (see the drawing below) about every 4 feet. This means our 15-foot-long building will require three collar ties. However, if you're building a loft, leave out the collar tie at that end, so you won't bang your head on it; the loft will be designed to take its place.

Step 1. On your sawhorses, cut two (or three if you're not installing a loft) 2×6s to 7 feet long.

Step 2. Cut off a 4″ by 9″ triangle from the upper corners of each 2×6.

Step 3. Start at least two 12d (not 16d) nails at each end of the collar tie. Drive the nails almost all the way through.

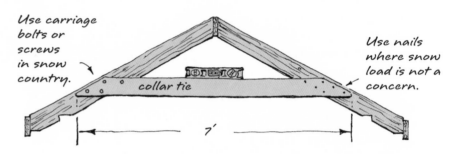

Use carriage bolts or screws in snow country.

collar tie

Use nails where snow load is not a concern.

7′

Step 4. With you and your friend at opposite ends, hold the collar tie to the pair of rafters, at about ¼″ to ½″ below the top edge of the rafters. Place your level on it, then both of you slide or nudge the tie until it's level.

Step 5. While your friend holds one end, take down the level and drive in the nails. Use five or six nails at each end.

Step 6. Once the collar ties are installed, remove the temporary wall ties.

Fastening Collar Ties

If you live in snow country, you may want to bolt or screw the ties to the rafters to handle the heavy snow load. Use 4″-long by ¼″-diameter carriage bolts or 3″-long construction screws. First, set up the tie to the rafters as before, again using your level. Tack the tie to the rafters with a 12d nail or two, or use a clamp to secure the tie to both rafters. For the bolts, get out your power drill, put in a ¼″ bit, and drill four holes through the tie and rafters. Knock in the bolts with your hammer, add a washer and a nut to each, and tighten them with a wrench. For the screws, use at least six at each end of the tie. Drill pilot holes, only through the first board, if necessary, and use your power drill to screw them in.

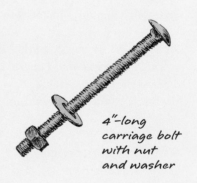

4″-long carriage bolt with nut and washer

INSTALL THE FASCIA BOARDS

Again, you'll need a friend and two stepladders.

Step 1. Put the two fascia boards you marked up earlier on your sawhorses. From the unmarked or outside of each board, start a 16d galvanized box nail opposite the X for each rafter.

Step 2. With a friend holding one end, lift a fascia board into place. Check that the edge lines on the inside of the board line up with the rafter ends and that its top edge sits about ¾″ below the rafter tails, and then nail the fascia board to the rafter tails. (Positioning the fascia board below the rafter tails will allow an even surface for the sheathing.) Start nailing at one end, pulling the fascia board up or down a bit as you proceed, to align it properly with every rafter. Drive two or three nails through the fascia board into every rafter tail.

Step 3. Repeat with the other fascia board.

INSTALL THE OVERHANG RAFTERS

Once the fascia boards are nailed on, have your friend help you put up those four overhang rafters, sometimes called barge boards, that you set aside earlier. If they fit snugly between the fascia board and the ridge board, they should automatically be in line with the other rafters.

Step 1. While your friend helps you hold the barge board in place, drive in the nail you started on the fascia board into the bottom of each rafter.

Step 2. Toenail the upper end of the barge board into the ridge board with 6d or 8d nails. You're hanging out in space here a bit, so be patient.

Take a long break, sit in the sun, have a banana . . . you've just completed the most difficult part of this journey.

Installing the Roofing

To lift the large panels of sheathing onto your roof, you'll need an extension ladder and a friend. Take your time with this until you get used to moving around on a sloped roof.

INSTALL THE SHEATHING

Step 1. Set a full sheet of ½"-thick plywood or OSB somewhere along one fascia board, aligning it so that any inner edges sit in the middle of rafters, leaving nailing room for other sheets of sheathing. You can set it at the end of the roof or in the middle. Tack it down with some 6d or 7d nails.

Step 2. Measure and cut other pieces of plywood or OSB to complete this first course of sheathing to the ends of the roof. Once they look good, nail on this first course of panels.

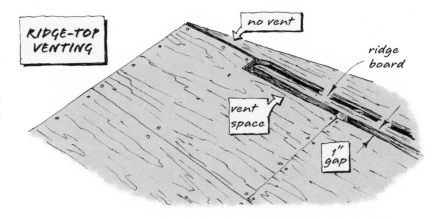

Step 3. Measure and cut the next course of sheathing to extend to the top of the ridge. Leave a 1½" gap between the ridge board and the top edge of the sheathing *except* where the sheathing extends beyond the walls (see the drawing above). This will allow for ventilation in your roof. Stagger the seams in the courses of panels so they meet at different rafters, then nail them on.

Step 4. Repeat on the other side. You're getting there!

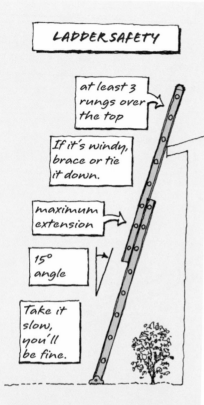

LADDER SAFETY

at least 3 rungs over the top

If it's windy, brace or tie it down.

maximum extension

15° angle

Take it slow, you'll be fine.

Extension Ladder Safety

Now is a good time to talk about using extension ladders. You'll need a sturdy, lightweight extension ladder to safely work on your roof. Set it on solid ground that won't sink or shift under the ladder feet. Lean it at about 15° (see the drawing above), and tie it to your wall or roof framing with rope or bungee cords if it's a windy day. Climb the ladder slowly at first until you get the feel of it. Trust the ladder and your sense of balance and you'll be fine.

PUT ON THE ROOFING

For your roofing, you'll first lay down 15-pound felt roofing underlayment, generally called tar paper, then a metal drip edge all around the edges, and finally three-tab asphalt shingles in a color of your choice. You'll need a utility knife, a staple gun or hammer tacker, and tin snips along with your usual tools.

Step 1. Unroll the 15-pound felt on the ground, measure to 18 feet, and cut off a piece with your utility knife. Repeat this until you have four pieces.

Step 2. Roll up one piece, carry it to the roof, and unroll it from one end along the bottom of your roof. Tack it down using a staple gun or, if you don't have a staple gun or hammer tacker, roofing nails. If you are going to shingle over it right away, you'll need only a few staples (or roofing nails) to hold down the underlayment. Use more on the exposed edges if it's windy. Trim off the excess felt at the gable ends with your utility knife.

Step 3. Repeat with the next piece, overlapping the first course by at least 4". Cut away any felt that covers the ridge-top vent.

Step 4. Repeat on the other side.

Note: Do not walk on the roofing felt until you've tacked it down — it might slide out from under you.

APPLY THE DRIP EDGE

Now it's time to apply the drip edge, which will protect your roof edges from the weather. (If you want to cover the end rafters with a wide trim board, though, which is nice looking but optional, do that first; see the box on facing page.) It might be easiest to nail on the drip edge from a ladder, rather than from the roof. You'll need a pair of tin snips (or heavy-duty kitchen shears) to cut the drip edge.

Step 1. Place your first piece of drip edge on the lowest edge of the roof. Use roofing nails to nail through the top part of the drip edge.

Step 2. Working from the bottom to the top of the roof, continue to nail on the edging, overlapping the pieces by about 3".

Step 3. When you reach the ridge top, cut the vertical part of the L-shaped drip edge at the ridge, then bend the top of the drip edge over the peak of the roof to get a nice-looking finish.

Trimming the Roof

For a clean look at the ends of your roof, you can cover the end rafters with 1×8 cedar or pine trim boards. If you decide to do this, put them up before you nail on the drip edge (see the drawing at right).

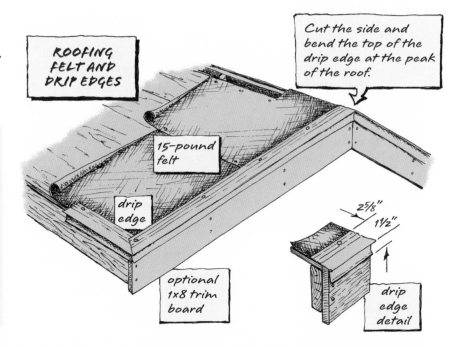

ROOFING FELT AND DRIP EDGES

Cut the side and bend the top of the drip edge at the peak of the roof.

15-pound felt

drip edge

optional 1×8 trim board

2⅝" 1½"

drip edge detail

SHINGLE THE ROOF

Set a package of your three-tab shingles on a plank on your sawhorses, and carefully read the directions on the package. You can easily cut asphalt roofing by scoring it on the back with your utility knife against a steel straightedge and then snapping the pieces apart. These are the basic steps for standard three-tab roofing shingles.

HOW TO APPLY THREE-TAB ROOF SHINGLES

Step 1. For the starter course, cut off all the tabs from about five pieces of three-tab roofing. Save these tabs because you can use them to cover the ridge of your roof. Nail the starter-course pieces to your roof, lined up on the edge of your drip edging.

continued on next page

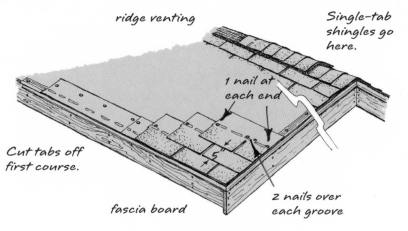

ridge venting

Single-tab shingles go here.

1 nail at each end

Cut tabs off first course.

fascia board

2 nails over each groove

Step 2. Stagger the next course by one-half of a shingle tab, and set it to reveal a 5-inch exposure, which will have the tabs just covering the grooves of the course below. Drive two ¾" or 1" roofing nails 2" apart and about ¾" above each groove and a single nail at the ends (see the drawing on page 189).

Step 3. Continue with your shingle courses, setting and nailing them in a staggered pattern. Trim the ends of each shingle course cleanly at the edge of your drip edges.

Step 4. When you get to the top, trim the shingles to keep the vent gap clear.

Step 5. Get your ridge venting, and set it in place according to the directions. Different brands vary on how they are applied, but most allow shingle tabs to be applied over the venting for a finished look.

Step 6. Nail or glue on your cut-off or single-shingle tabs to cover the ridge.

PUT IN A SOFFIT

With this roof design, you will need to cover the outside space under your roof, called the eaves, with a board called a soffit.

Step 1. Using tin snips, cut out 3"-wide strips of hardware cloth for vent mesh. Stretch these along the underside of your rafters (as shown in the drawing at right), and attach them with roofing nails. This is the lower vent for your roof, and the mesh will keep the bugs out.

Step 2. Holding a small level to each rafter tail, make a mark on the wall across from it with your pencil. Continue until you have a row of marks level with the bottoms of the rafters.

Step 3. Nail a 1×3 furring strip above the marks, to hold your soffit board. Use a 6d or 8d nail every 12" (see the drawing at right).

Step 4. Get out your 1×8 soffit boards, and use them to cover the underside of the overhang. Cut the boards so they join midway across a rafter tail, so each board has a solid surface to be nailed to. There should be a 1"- to 2"-wide gap revealing the wire mesh for the soffit venting.

Step 5. Nail up the soffit boards with 6d or 7d galvanized box nails. You'll be nailing upside down, which can be challenging. If you think it will be easier, you can use 1⅝" or 2"-long galvanized construction screws and your drill.

Hey, your roof is roofed!

PUTTING IN A SOFFIT

soffit

vent mesh

fascia board

CHAPTER 12

FINISHING UP

With the walls and roof framed and covered, now it can rain all day and your place will stay dry — until the wind picks up. So you need to finish closing it up. To do this, I'll show you how to build the walls in the gable ends and then put in the windows and the door.

Once your shelter is closed up, you'll want to add the finishing touches to make this hideaway your own. I'll talk about installing siding and trim for the outside, building a loft, and finishing the inside with wood or drywall. I'll also include a note about wiring your place for lighting and electrical outlets.

For more ideas and discussion about different siding materials, landscaping, planting, and patio trellises, see chapter 7.

Finishing the Gable-End Walls

Get your stepladder and look at the still-open gable-end space under the rafters. Here you'll put in some short 2×4 studs from the top plate up to the rafters, and then you can cover the remaining wall framing. Use leftover 2×4s and sheathing from your wall construction for these gable-end walls.

INSTALL STUDS IN THE GABLE-END WALLS

The studs in the gable space will line up directly above the studs in the wall below.

Step 1. Measuring from the wall corners, mark 16" centerlines, then edge lines, along the top plate.

Step 2. Next, use a level or plumb bob to mark edge lines for those same studs where they will attach to the rafters. Mark the edge lines on the rafter at the longer or higher edge of the stud location.

Step 3. Measure the distance from the edge line on the rafter down to the top of the plate to find the length for each stud, as shown on facing page.

Step 4. Cut the studs with angled notches to fit under the rafters. To find the angle cut for the notch, set your square on the edge of a 2×4, just as you did on the rafters — it's the same 6:12 pitch — and make the cut mark. To cut out the notch, clamp down the 2×4 and saw the long leg of the notch with your power saw. Then with your handsaw, cut out the angled notch. Cut off the bottom or square end last. The unnotched leg remaining is 4" long for all the angled studs.

Step 5. Toenail the stud into the plate and into the rafter with 6d nails, or through the rafter with 12d or 16d nails. (These little studs bounce around, so use the nails that work best for you.)

Step 6. On the gable end of wall 3, arrange the studs around the window frame as shown on facing page.

Now you can finish covering the gable-end walls with plywood or OSB. Cut sheathing pieces that will tie the window header and the rafter together. Use 7d or 8d coated sinkers to fasten it. For strong gable ends, especially over a wide window, apply construction adhesive to the stud edges before you nail on the sheathing.

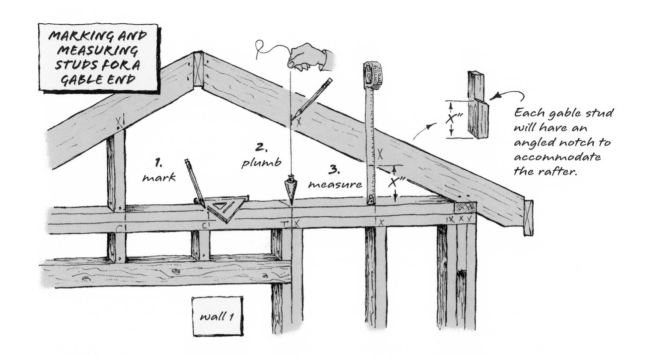

MARKING AND MEASURING STUDS FOR A GABLE END

1. mark

2. plumb

3. measure

wall 1

Each gable stud will have an angled notch to accommodate the rafter.

NOTCHING A GABLE-END STUD

1. Mark the angle cut on the stud.

4"

2. Make the long vertical cut.

1½"
4"

3. Make the short angled cut.

WALL 3 GABLE END

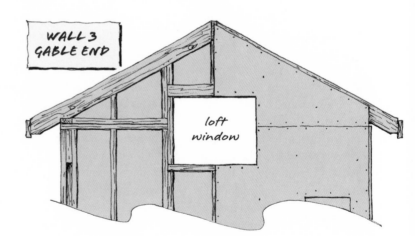

loft window

Installing the Windows and Door

The right windows and doors can make an architectural gem out of the most humble shelter. Conversely, with the wrong scale or size, they can make it look like an ungainly shed. Take some time to look around, and the right windows and door will come to you.

You can order new window units, such as horizontal sliders or casement windows, or you can build your own frames around recycled windows, barn sash, or custom-ordered windowpanes. In this example, we will build window frames to fit windows already on hand. The windows can then be hinged or fixed into the frames — it's your choice. You can also install your windows clubhouse style, without the frames, as shown in chapter 5.

New framed window units are relatively easy to put in, but you will still need to add trim boards around them for a good look. Unfortunately, off-the-shelf window units are plain looking (i.e., boring) and scaled for bigger structures — like houses. Unless you're willing to spend a lot of money for custom-designed windows, I recommend building your own frames around old-style new or used windows.

One more alternative: You can custom-order relatively inexpensive and energy-efficient double-glazed windowpanes. Local glass-supply stores can have these glass-only (no frame) panels made for you to your exact size requirements. You would then install them as "fixed" windows without hinges.

As for a door, I recommend a quality exterior prehung, or already framed, door. A 30"-wide by 80"-tall door would be a good fit for your shelter. It helps to have thought about how you'll finish your interior walls before buying a prehung exterior door.

At the lumberyard, ask for a prehung 2/6 exterior door. The 2/6 means the door itself is 2 feet 6 inches wide (30"). Ask for a frame or jamb that is $4\frac{9}{16}$" wide if you'll use $\frac{1}{2}$"-thick drywall or $4\frac{13}{16}$" wide if you'll use $\frac{3}{4}$"-thick pine paneling inside. The lumberyard staff can then show you their catalog of door styles that is almost endless, so find a door that you like.

Also, before you order a prehung door, determine which direction you'll want it to open: right-hand or left-hand. For a left-hand door, as you stand *outside* the door, the knob will be on the *right*, and the door will swing *away* from you, *to your left*. A right-hand door will do the reverse. You may have to explain this to the sales staff to get it right.

Door and Window Materials

Part	Quantity	Description
Window frames	10	1×6 boards, 8 feet or longer, "quality" or "no. 1" pine
Exterior window trim	10	1×4 boards, 10 to 12 feet long, cedar or redwood
Nails	2 pounds of each	8d finish nails; 6d or 8d galvanized box nails
Door	1	30″ × 80″, or 2/6, prehung, left-opening, exterior, with lockset (a doorknob that locks with a key)
Windows	varies	all openable windows will need two hinges and one latch each

It's Your Choice

As you've probably noticed by now, I tend to favor methods that give you the most value for your money. However, if you prefer guaranteed weather-tight and worry-free windows and you've found a custom design you like, then by all means spend what it takes and order something really nice. After all, you'll be living with your choice for many years. Install any factory-framed windows into your wall openings according to the manufacturer's instructions. Get a friend to help you set them in place — they can be heavy.

Putting in the Windows

Take time to find the right windows. It is easy to walk into a large home center and be dazzled by the sheer quantity of windows on display. Most will not look right on your shelter. Try to find a design that suits not only the size you need but also has some character, such as old-fashioned multipaned window styles, leaded windows, or even some with stained glass. Keep your eye out, and the right windows will appear.

In this example, you will build and install box frames around the windows. Before making your box frames, however, measure the window openings and your windows to make sure everything will fit as planned. The wall openings are designed to be 1″ bigger than the actual window all the way around. That allows for the ¾″-thick box frames and ¼″ wiggle room. Wiggle room allows space for adding shims to enable leveling of the window frame.

If the measurements look good, then you're ready to build the box frame.

BUILD AND INSTALL BOX WINDOW FRAME

You'll cut the box-frame pieces from 1×6 boards. In addition to being cut to length to form the box frame, the 1×6 boards will have to be cut lengthwise, or ripped, to fit into your walls nicely. The window frames should be 4⁹⁄₁₆″ wide if you'll use ½″-thick drywall inside, or 4¹³⁄₁₆″ wide if you'll use ¾″-thick pine paneling inside.

Step 1. Cut the 1×6 boards to the lengths and widths you need for your box frame (see page 202 if you need advice on using a rip fence with a power saw).

Step 2. Assemble the frame, as shown in the drawing below. Use three or four 6d or 8d box nails per corner.

Step 3. Slide the frame into the wall opening, and set it with shims so it will stay put. Using a level, adjust the shims as necessary to make the window frame both level and plumb.

Step 4. Adjust the outer edge of the frame to make it even or flush with the outside surface of the sheathing. When it's good, nail it in with 8d finish nails.

Step 5. Apply 1×4 trim to the outside of the window. Set these trim boards to overlap the inside of the frame edge by ½″ to hold the window in place (see the drawing below left). (Alternatively, you could nail the trim boards onto the frame on your sawhorses and then put it into the wall.) Nail the trim with 6d galvanized nails into the edge of the window frame, and with 6d or 8d galvanized box nails firmly into the wall around the window.

Step 6. Caulk the top of the top trim board, or use Z flashing, as shown at left.

BOX FRAME FOR A WINDOW

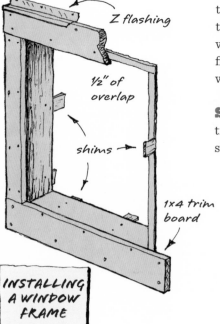

Z flashing

½″ of overlap

shims

1x4 trim board

INSTALLING A WINDOW FRAME

INSTALL THE WINDOW

If the window will be fixed (no hinges), fit it in the frame, and nail a 1×2 piece of trim or furring strip into the frame all around the inside of the window. Outside, caulk the window all around where it meets the exterior trim boards. If the window will be openable, follow these steps:

Step 1. Set the window on your sawhorses and attach a thin metal rain shield to its outside bottom edge. You can make this shield by trimming and then bending a flat strip of aluminum flashing, which is sold in rolls and used for weather protection. Use tin snips or kitchen shears to cut it. You could also use a piece of Z flashing, with its bottom part bent up.

Step 2. Test the length to get as close a fit as possible, then attach it to your window frame by gently pounding in 1"-long copper brads (tiny nails) or use round-headed wood screws. Caulk or seal the top edge of the metal to the wood. This will help keep out the rain.

Step 3. Set the window into the frame, and shim it so it is plumb and level and doesn't scrape the floor of the frame.

Step 4. Attach the hinges, following the instructions on page 85.

Step 5. Finally, attach a twist latch, called a casement latch, to the window, which will close it tightly.

WINDOW RAIN SHIELD

inside

metal rain shield

outside

FINISHED WINDOW

outside

inside

half-opening, half-fixed double window

Putting in the Door

Here is a cart-before-the-horse situation: It is wise to have the door on hand, or its specific rough-opening requirements, before you frame the wall opening. This project uses the standard rough-opening size (called RO in carpenter-speak) of 2″ wider and 2½″ higher than the actual door size, but some prehung doors may require a different rough opening.

Your prehung door will probably arrive all wrapped up. First, check to see if it is the size you ordered and that it opens in the direction you asked for. Find the installation instructions and read them carefully. You'll likely be installing the door frame together with the door into the wall opening. Have a friend help you set the door in place. Use shims to set it plumb and level, and tack it in place with nails, as instructed by the manufacturer. Also check to see that it is flush with the outside sheathing surface.

Prehung exterior doors often include an outside trim board, usually called "brick molding." This will work fine, but you can also replace it with your 1×4 or other trim if you prefer. Most prehung doors come with holes drilled for the doorknob, or lockset, and many recommend the brand of lockset that is compatible with the drilled holes. This is good. Choose a style of lockset that you like for your door, and install it as described by the instructions.

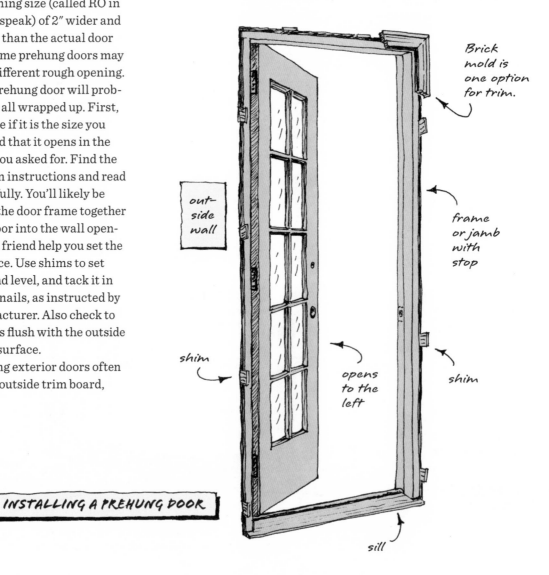

Brick mold is one option for trim.

outside wall

frame or jamb with stop

shim

opens to the left

shim

sill

INSTALLING A PREHUNG DOOR

HOW TO BUILD YOUR OWN DOOR FRAME

If you have found the perfect recycled door and want to build a frame or jamb for it, like the window frame just described, or if you've purchased an exterior door frame kit, follow these steps for putting the pieces together and installing the frame in your wall.

Step 1. Check your door to make sure it is square. Some old doors have had their tops or bottoms shaved off at angles to fit sloping floors. You may have to resaw the top or bottom with your power saw to square it.

Step 2. So that it will be flush with both the outside edge of the exterior sheathing and the inside finished wall, your door frame should be 4⁹⁄₁₆″ wide if you'll use ½″-thick drywall or 4¹³⁄₁₆″ wide if you'll use ¾″-thick pine paneling inside. If you're working with a kit, look for one in the appropriate width. If you're working without a kit, you'll need to rip 1×6 lumber to the appropriate width. Do that now; see page 202 for instruction on using a rip fence with a power saw. Cut pieces for the top and two sides of the frame. The bottom piece will be the threshold, a sturdy, slightly sloped board that fits just under the door and helps shed rain; you can buy wooden exterior thresholds at most lumberyards.

Step 3. You've checked your door and made it square, right? Now cut the top piece of your frame long enough to allow for the width of the door, the thickness of the two side pieces of the frame, and ⅛″ wiggle room. Cut the threshold just long enough to allow for the width of the door plus ⅛″; don't include the thickness of the side pieces in its length.

continued on next page

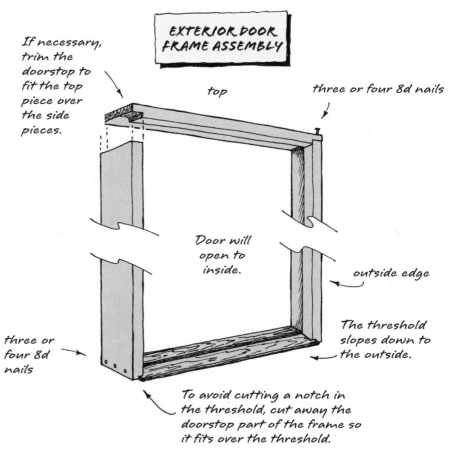

If necessary, trim the doorstop to fit the top piece over the side pieces.

EXTERIOR DOOR FRAME ASSEMBLY

top

three or four 8d nails

Door will open to inside.

outside edge

three or four 8d nails

The threshold slopes down to the outside.

To avoid cutting a notch in the threshold, cut away the doorstop part of the frame so it fits over the threshold.

Step 4. Nail the pieces together, as shown in the drawing on page 199. If the top piece and threshold of your door frame are built with a doorstop as one piece, trim the ends off the doorstop before assembling the frame, to accommodate the side pieces. Saw any extra wood off the door frame that extends below the underside of the threshold.

Step 5. Set the door frame in your rough opening, with its outside edge flush with the outside sheathing surface. If you bought an exterior door frame kit, check that the doorstop edge is facing outside, so that your door will open to the inside.

Step 6. The door frame should fit loosely in your rough opening, with the threshold resting on the floor. Use your level to make it square, and then use shims and a nail or two to hold it in place for nailing. Test the door by setting it in the frame. If it looks good, take out the door and nail in the frame. Use two 8d finish nails every 16" or so.

Step 7. Get a set of three 3" or 3½" butt hinges, with removable pins, which are made for doors. The hinges will need to be mortised, or set, into the edge of the door and into the frame, and they must be lined up for the door to hang properly. Use a hinge to mark its edges on the door for all the hinges. Take out the pins and separate the hinge halves.

Step 8. Set the door on edge on the floor, and chisel out the hinge mortises just deep enough so the hinge surface is level with the wood surface around it — go no deeper. Then mark the screw holes with the hinge half. Screw the hinge halves into the door, but not tightly.

Step 9. Set the door in the frame, and mark the hinge edges on the door frame. Remove the door. Carve out the space for the hinges as you did on the door, and screw the hinge halves into the frame, but not tightly.

Step 10. Hang the door by joining the hinge halves. Tap the pins into the hinges, and tighten up all the screws. This always takes more time than I like, but it works.

Step 11. If your old door doesn't already have a doorknob or lockset, install your doorknob hardware according to the instructions, if available. Chisel out a striker-plate hole for the door latch into the frame, and install a striker plate.

Step 12. Add a doorstop (but skip this step if you used a door frame kit with a doorstop included); you can find pine doorstops at most lumberyards. Cut the strips to size. Close the door gently so it is latched, then draw a line all around the door frame to determine the edge of your doorstop. Using 4d finish nails, nail the doorstop, which will also help provide a weather seal around the door, into your frame. All this can be done after the door is hung.

All this carving, fitting, and futzing can get frustrating, so be patient, turn up your boombox, and relax. It is your choice, of course, to build your own frame or simply buy a prehung door.

Building a Loft

Now it's time to build the loft. The loft will also help tie the walls together, so if you decide *not* to build it, then add one more collar tie to your rafters (see page 185). You will need your usual tools, a stepladder, and these materials:

Loft Materials

Part	Quantity	Description
Loft beams	3	2×6s, 8 feet long
Loft joists	7	2×4s, 6 feet long
Loft floor	9	1×8 car siding boards, 8 feet long; *or*
	12	1×6 car siding boards, 8 feet long
Screws	1 pound	2½"-long construction screws
Nails	1 pound of each	16d coated sinkers; 8d finish nails

Ladder and Railing Materials

Part	Quantity	Description
Ladder rails	2	2×6s, 8 feet long
Ladder steps	1	⁵⁄₄×6 cedar decking board, 10 feet long (to be cut into five steps, each 21½" long)
Railing	1	⁵⁄₄×6 cedar decking board, 6 feet long
Spindles	3	pine 2×2s, 8 feet long (to be cut into twelve 23½" railing spindles)

CUT THE JOIST SUPPORT PIECES

The loft frame and floor will be supported by two beams. Each beam is made of a 2×6 and a joist support piece, joined in an L formation. The rear beam will be 7 feet 5 inches (89") long and the front beam will be 8 feet long. (Though you can shorten these lengths a bit if the beams fit too tightly.) You'll rip the joist support pieces from an 8-foot-long 2×6 using a power saw and a rip fence, which should be included with the power saw kit.

Step 1. The two joist support pieces are exactly 2" wide. So, start by using your tape measure to set the rip fence blade 2" from the face of the saw blade, then tighten the fence screw. Draw a short cut line 2" from the edge of the 2×6, to confirm the rip-fence position when you start cutting.

Step 2. Clamp an 8-foot-long 2×6 to your sawhorses. The saw will want to tip over while you are cutting, so set another 2×6 or a 2×4 over your sawhorses to help support the saw.

Step 3. Begin the cut. Guide the saw slowly as you get used to keeping the fence snug to the edge of the board. If it wanders, turn off the saw, back it up, and then recut it straight.

Step 4. Flip the cut 2×6 over, so that you can run your saw along the remaining straight factory-cut side, and cut another 2"-wide piece from the board. Now you have two joist support pieces.

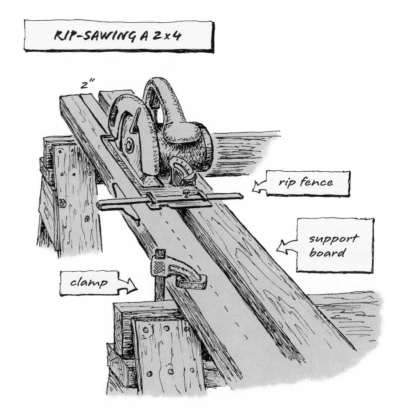

RIP-SAWING A 2×4

2"

rip fence

support board

clamp

INSTALL THE FRONT AND REAR BEAMS

For a stronger building, the loft beams will be firmly attached to the wall framing. The outer edge of the front beam will extend to 4 feet 9 inches (57") from the rear wall.

Step 1. Measure from the rear wall along both side walls to 57", and mark the floor at that spot.

Step 2. On both side walls, the mark should fall between a pair of studs. Between these studs, attach a 2×6 block to support the loft beam, setting it so that its top is 66" up from the floor. (For extra strength, you can add a support stud under it, which should be about 59" long.)

Step 3. Measure again from the end wall to exactly 57", and draw a line across the top of each 2×6 block at this spot. These lines mark the position of the outside edge of the front beam. Set the beam in place, aligning its outer edge with the lines you just drew. Then add another 2×4 block, laid flat, on top of the beam to better tie it to the wall (see the drawing below).

Step 4. Attach one of the 2"-wide joist support pieces to the inside face of the front beam. I recommend using 2½"-long construction screws, set about 12" apart. For easier screwing, first drill ⅛" pilot holes through the 2"-wide joist support piece.

Step 5. On the rear wall, measure 66" up from the floor, and draw a horizontal line across the studs. Tack a couple of 16d nails to this line, then rest the 2×6 rear beam on these nails to hold it in the right place. Nail or screw the 2×6 directly into all the studs it meets. Use at least two 16d nails or 2½" screws per stud.

Step 6. Attach the remaining 2"-wide ripped joist support piece to this beam, as you did for the front beam.

ATTACHING LOFT BEAM

existing wall

tie-in and support blocks

2x4

loft beam

2x6

optional support stud

2x6

INSTALL THE JOISTS

Step 1. Measure and cut seven 2×4s to fit snugly between the loft beams, resting on the joist support pieces between the beams.

Step 2. Set the two end joists in place, and fasten them in place by driving 16d nails directly through the joists into the studs on the side walls. Then set the remaining joists in place, spacing them evenly across the loft floor frame (at about 14¾" center-to-center).

Step 3. For a clean look, without nail heads exposed on the outside of the front loft beam, toenail each joist with only one 6d or 8d nail through the top of the joist and into the beam. The 2"-wide support pieces will otherwise hold the joists in place.

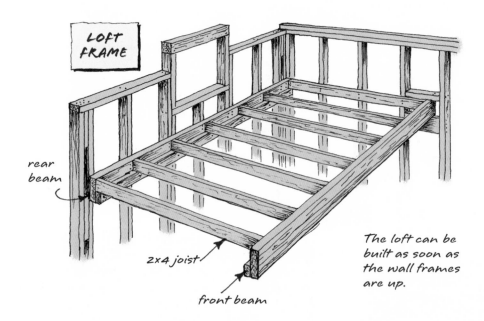

LOFT FRAME

rear beam

2x4 joist

front beam

The loft can be built as soon as the wall frames are up.

ADD THE FLOOR, RAILINGS, AND ACCESS LADDER

Step 1. For your loft floor, lay down car siding, with the grooves facing down, or some other ¾"-thick pine boards. Start at the back wall, and work forward toward the loft edge. Use 8d finish nails, two or three per joist, and use your nail set to avoid dinging the loft floor with your hammer. When you get to the last board, you'll probably need to rip it to width (the same way you did for the loft beam; see page 202). After nailing it in place, plane or sand its edge for a smooth, finished look.

Step 2. Next, build a ladder so you can get up to your loft. You can build an access ladder with rungs, but for a more comfortable ladder, build it with flat steps instead, as shown in the drawing below.

Step 3. Finally, build a railing by attaching spindles every 4″ to sections of ⁵⁄₄×6 cedar decking. With a friend's help, attach the assembled railing to the deck beam, as shown below with two 2½″-long screws per spindle.

FINDING THE ANGLE ON A SPEED SQUARE

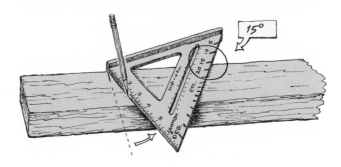

15°

LOFT LADDER & RAILING

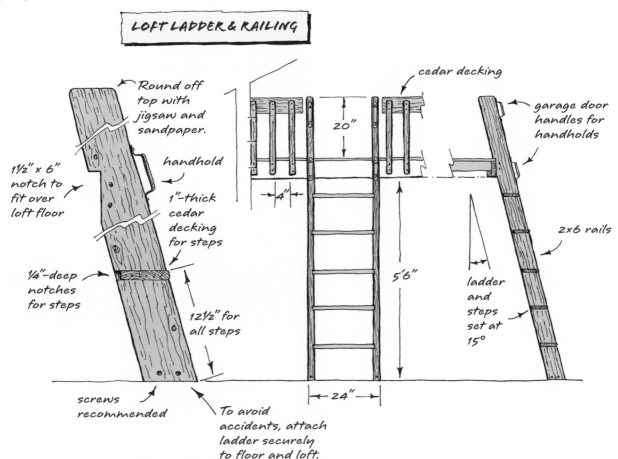

Round off top with jigsaw and sandpaper.

cedar decking

handhold

1½″ x 6″ notch to fit over loft floor

1″-thick cedar decking for steps

¼″-deep notches for steps

12½″ for all steps

garage door handles for handholds

2x6 rails

ladder and steps set at 15°

20″

4″

5′6″

24″

screws recommended

To avoid accidents, attach ladder securely to floor and loft.

CECIL'S CHRISTMAS PRESENT

In the fall of 1991 Merrall MacNeille, a house designer in Massachusetts, began building what he told his daughter, Cecil, was to be a chicken coop. Merrall tells this wonderful Christmas story of how the coop, on a cold December night, was magically transformed into a girl's dream playhouse. His drawings are as exquisite as his end product, revealing Merrall's love of art in architecture as well as his joy of building.

" It was below zero and a week before Christmas when we started the playhouse. We had been accumulating materials for years. The heavy wood we used mostly came from old buildings being demolished in the area. By Christmas Eve, we had a nice 'chicken house' started; the floor, walls, flat ceiling, and the door were already in place. The kids had been working hard (pulling nails mostly), but then it dropped to –18°F, too cold for children.

In the ensuing 24 hours, St. Nicholas transformed the chicken house into a playhouse! In Cecil's stocking was a map locating the playhouse and then a secret panel inside, where her presents were hidden. She walked out, following the map (in that bitter cold), and found a little house with a bay window and a window seat, a wood cookstove, casement windows, a ladder and a trapdoor to a loft, and a porch. Later came the finished roof with finials on the ridge salvaged from an old tenement in Holyoke. I built it for less than $500.

Cecil has furnished the house and lives in it most of the summer, coming in for an occasional meal and to replenish the ice chest. An Igloo cooler provides running water, and hot water is provided by a kettle on the stove, fired by the dried applewood from our old orchard."

— *Merrall MacNeille*

SECTION

SIDE

FRONT

·CECIL'S PLAYHOUSE· ·KENDALL MACNEILLE· 11/7/91

Installing Trim and Siding

Take some time to think about the exterior look of your shelter. Do you want it to match a bigger house nearby or to fit your own vision of a personal place? Traditional wood siding is extensively covered in chapter 7 (see page 104), but other materials such as stucco and unique items such as recycled doors are also worth considering. The trim materials listed below will work with the traditional sidings.

Trim and Siding Materials

Part	Quantity	Description
Weather barrier	400 square feet	housewrap or 15-pound felt
Trim	12	1×4s, 12 feet long, cedar or redwood
Trim	3	1×6s, 12 feet long, cedar or redwood (optional; see trim drawing on facing page)
Siding	360 square feet	your choice of material and style
Nails	1 pound	7d or 8d galvanized box nails (for trim)
Nails	5 pounds	6d or 8d galvanized box or siding nails (for siding)
Sealant	2 tubes	paintable acrylic or silicone exterior caulk

Wrapping the Walls

Before installing the trim and siding, wrap your shelter with a semipermeable, protective layer of plastic. Commonly called housewrap, this material comes in wide rolls and keeps rain out while releasing moisture from inside the house. For wood siding, ask for the ribbed design, which doesn't trap moisture behind the boards as much as the smooth variety. Or use 15-pound felt roofing underlayment (tar paper) for the same purpose. Have a friend help you put up the wrap, then tack it on using a staple gun.

Putting Up the Trim

A good trim material is 1×4 cedar. Cedar cuts easily, won't shrink or crack as much as pine, and will hold up to the weather a long time. Use your handsaw to cut it if you find the circular saw strays too much from your cut line. Nail it on with 7d or 8d galvanized box nails.

Take the time to fit the wall trim boards carefully, especially at the gable ends. Cut the angles under the gable-end roof at the same 6:12 pitch as you did the rafter ends. The drawing at right suggests wide trim boards under the window and roof overhang, but feel free to alter the width any way you'd like. Use pieces of cedar or exterior knot-free plywood to cover the soffit ends.

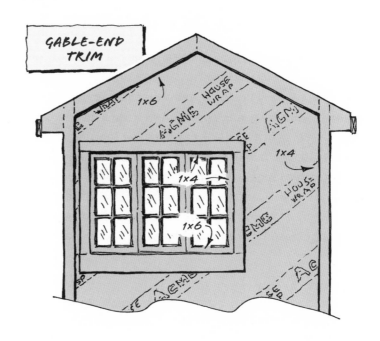

GABLE-END TRIM

Putting Up the Siding

See chapter 7 for a thorough discussion of siding options. And don't forget recycled siding; new wood siding isn't cheap! If you find someone replacing their pine or cedar siding with plastic, ask if you can salvage their old boards. They will likely be delighted to give them to you to save Dumpster costs. Salvage yards and the ReStore might also have recycled wood siding. You may have to remove some loose paint, but a possible unique look, and the low cost, may make this worth it.

For good weather protection, caulk any minor gaps between boards and the joints where the siding meets the edges of trim boards, especially around the windows and door. Acrylic or silicone caulk with long-lasting flexibility is best. Quality cedar shingles and trim can take the weather without being painted, but other raw wood sidings should be stained or painted after the caulking is completed.

Now your place is weather-tight. Pop a cork; you deserve it!

Installing Plumbing, Wiring, and Heating

The next step is to decide how you want to arrange the inside of your place. If you want a kitchen or a sink, this will mean installing plumbing. If you want hot water, you can add an electric flash heater to your water line. To get water, you can run an underground water pipe from your house, or even use a garden hose to connect to your household water source. The sink can drain out to your own "gray water" system, which is essentially a buried container of gravel that helps the ground absorb your sink's wastewater. I suggest a portable toilet for bathroom needs. Common on boats and RVs, this self-contained device can be periodically emptied into a regular toilet. A small composting toilet vented to the outside may also work, as long as it does not exceed 13″ wide by 18″ long.

Will you want electricity? If so, for what? If you are thinking about food, then you will need outlets for a microwave and mini-fridge. Will you want a lamp by the bed, and power for your computer, entertainment system, or the lava lamp collection? Will you have lights in the ceiling or outside? Will you want cable?

Electrical needs will mean running wire through your walls. In houses, the electrical power comes from the utility company to a breaker panel, or breaker box. In your backyard shelter, the power will likely come from the main breaker panel in your house to a smaller breaker panel, or subpanel, in the shelter.

You can legally install electrical circuits, outlets, and fixtures yourself, since this is your place. However, I recommend finding someone experienced in wiring complete circuits, including the subpanel, to help you install it. Once you've seen it done, it will be easy, but there are safety requirements to consider.

The final consideration before you finish your walls is heating. For a shelter this size, a small wall-mounted ventless gas heater will most efficiently do the job. Electric heaters or baseboard heaters are also available, but most of these require 220-volt wiring. If you prefer a small wood-burning heater or fireplace, determine how you will install it, including a chimney and surrounding tilework or other heat barrier, before you finish your walls.

Now that your wiring, outlet and light boxes, plumbing, and a heater are all roughed in, as the builders say, you can finish your interior.

Adding Insulation

If you want to keep your shelter warm when it's cold and keep it cool when it's hot, consider insulation. The roof of this project has been designed to accept R-11 fiberglass insulation, which will allow 2″ of free air space for ventilation. R-19 (6″) insulation will fill up all of your vent space, which may cause mold or rot to form inside your roof. Since you set the rafters on 16″ centers, get the 14½″-wide rolls. Use the same R-11 rolls for the walls.

For the walls and ceiling, cut the insulation strips with your utility knife to the length you need. Fill all the spaces, including the narrow gaps between close-together studs. Use a staple gun to attach the reinforced paper edges of the insulation to the outer edges or sides of your studs and rafters (see the drawing at right).

For the final insulating step, and this one is optional, stretch thin polyurethane sheeting over your walls and ceiling, and staple it down. This will help keep moisture from sweating inside your walls during cold weather and hold in a bit more heat.

FIBERGLASS INSULATION

Staple to side of studs.

Cut to fit with utility knife.

Finishing Your Walls and Ceiling

For the interior finish, I suggest using pine paneling or a combination of paneling and drywall. Tongue-and-groove pine car siding, or knotty pine, depending on the style, is a beautiful and inexpensive natural wood that you can stain, varnish, or paint. It is best to apply pine boards horizontally, or across the studs, on the walls or ceiling. A balance of pine paneling and painted drywall can create a natural yet restful look.

Installing Pine Paneling

To put up 1×6 or 1×8 pine paneling such as car siding, cut the ends cleanly by using your square and a utility knife to score the cut line instead of drawing it with a pencil. Saw it with a sharp toolbox saw. For ripping, or cutting a board lengthwise, use your power saw and rip fence as shown on page 202. Nail in the boards with 8d finish nails, then, to avoid hammer dimples, set each nail with your nail set.

Hanging Drywall

The interior wall covering used by most house builders is drywall, which is also called plasterboard, wallboard, Sheetrock, or gypsum board. It is inexpensive and durable, and it can give a small room an elegant look. The standard 4-foot by 8-foot by ½"-thick drywall sheets are heavy, so ask a friend to help you put them up.

Finishing or plastering drywall can be challenging, but with a bit of practice, you can handle it. Also, store drywall out of the weather — rain will ruin it.

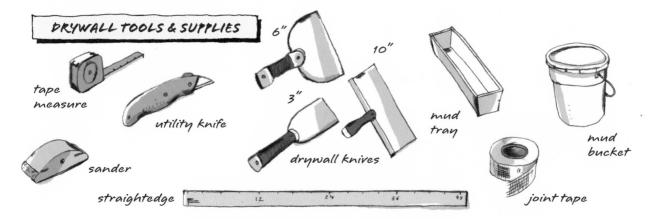

DRYWALL TOOLS & SUPPLIES

tape measure

utility knife

sander

3"

6"

10"

drywall knives

mud tray

mud bucket

joint tape

straightedge

HOW TO CUT DRYWALL

The following are some general tips for cutting drywall. You will need your tape measure, pencil, a utility knife, and a straight board or steel straightedge at least 48″ long.

Step 1. Measure and draw your cut line, using the straightedge. Cut through the surface paper with your knife along the cut line.

Step 2. Snap the sheet at the cut.

Step 3. Turn the sheet over, and cut through the back layer of paper.

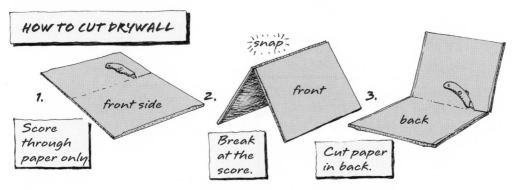

HOW TO CUT DRYWALL

1. *front side* — Score through paper only

snap — 2. *front* — Break at the score.

3. *back* — Cut paper in back.

HOW TO HANG DRYWALL

Get a friend to help you hang your drywall, especially on the ceiling. Use 1¼″-long drywall screws or nails for the walls, and 1⅝″-long drywall screws or nails for the ceiling. I recommend screws. To use drywall screws, get a special drywall-screw driver bit for your power drill. This inexpensive wonder sets the screws to the correct depth, making screwing easy.

Hang the large pieces of drywall first to minimize cutting. Save all the scraps, and then use them to fill in the smallest places. Especially when you're working with large pieces of drywall, which can be heavy, it's helpful to have a friend to help you hold them in place.

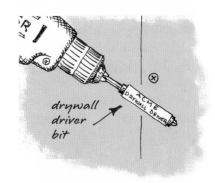

drywall driver bit

Step 1. Set a piece of drywall in place. Make sure all the edges of the piece will sit over studs or other solid framing, leaving room for attaching other pieces of drywall to the studs if necessary. If the drywall extends down to the floor, leave a ¼″ to ½″ gap at the base, for easier fastening; a trim board or baseboard will cover the gap later.

Step 2. Fasten the drywall to the framing, driving a screw (or nail) every 6″ on the edges and every 12″ on any inside studs.

HOW TO FINISH DRYWALL

After the drywall is up, you'll want to plaster the joints and the indentations, or dimples, made by the screws or nails. You'll need some drywall spatulas or knives, a roll of mesh-style joint tape, a bucket of drywall joint compound, and a mud tray.

Step 1. Check all the screws or nails to make sure the heads are flush or slightly "dimpled" into the drywall. Then lay down self-sticking 2"-wide mesh tape over the joints, and press it evenly into inside corner joints.

Step 2. Open the bucket of joint compound and stir it. Use a 3"-wide spatula to scoop out some joint compound, or mud, and plop it into the tray. While holding the tray in one hand, spread joint compound over the tape with a 6" knife, working it into the joint.

Step 3. Using a 9"- or 10"-wide knife, smooth out the compound in long, firm strokes, removing ridges, air holes, and other irregularities. Feather out the compound at its edges.

Step 4. Add one or two thin finish coats after your first layer dries. Use your 3"-wide knife to cover all the nail or screw heads with compound, at least twice.

Step 5. After the compound dries, sand it to remove any ridges or rough spots. When it all looks smooth enough to you, it's done.

One time-saving note: To avoid a lot of masking, prime and paint the drywall *before* you add any trim boards, paneling, or the finish flooring.

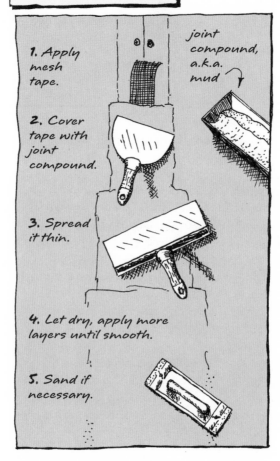

FINISHING DRYWALL

1. Apply mesh tape.

2. Cover tape with joint compound.

joint compound, a.k.a. mud

3. Spread it thin.

4. Let dry, apply more layers until smooth.

5. Sand if necessary.

Finishing the Floor and Trim

You can sand and paint the rough floorboards if you like (see chapter 7). Or you can install finished flooring, following the manufacturer's instructions.

If you want a reasonably priced, resilient, and easy-to-install finished floor, I suggest vinyl plank flooring. You don't need any glue or special tools, and the planks can be laid directly over your OSB subfloor, no matter how rough that has become during your construction. A few area rugs here and there will also warm things up.

Trimming It Out

After your floor is finished, you can add baseboards along the floor and trim boards around your door and windows. The simplest trim method is to use 1×3 or 1×4 pine boards, which will look good with your pine paneling.

Prepaint the Trim

If you are going to paint your trim a different color than the walls, prime and paint all the trim boards on your sawhorses before nailing them in. Then you only need to touch up the nail heads, thus avoiding a lot of messy masking tape.

HOW TO INSTALL TRIM

Step 1. Cut the boards to size as needed. The simplest way is to cut the boards square at the ends, but a neater, more elegant look can be had by mitering them, or cutting them at a 45°. For easy square or miter cuts, use a miter box and your handsaw.

Step 2. Plane and sand the long exposed edges for a splinter-free, finished look.

Step 3. With your smaller hammer, nail in the trim with 6d or 8d finish nails. Begin around the door, since the baseboard ends will later meet the sides of the door trim. Countersink the nail heads with your nail set.

Step 4. Cover up the sunken nail heads with wood filler. (You can find filler in just about any color to match your wood.) Use a flat-head screwdriver or butter knife to fill the holes, then rub off any excess with a rag.

Changing and Improving

Your place is finished . . . almost. Now you might want to build a partition for a tiny bathroom, closet, or private alcove. Frame it as you did the outside walls, and cover it with pine or drywall. You can also install or buy cabinets and shelves, add a nice rug, and maybe add a deck, patio, or hot tub outside. So many possibilities!

It's time to enjoy what you've done, and you certainly deserve it. Put out the patio chairs and call me when the hot tub is ready!

AMY'S TREE FORT WITHOUT THE TREE

In the hills near Greenland, New Hampshire, Don Cook built this sturdy "tree fort" for his daughter, Amy. The bouncy 2″ by 12″ plank bridge seems like great fun if you are 12 years old or younger. Adults need not even try, and that's just fine with the kids.

> " As a child, I continually had a tree house or a fort under construction. My father was very skilled with tools and was continuously remodeling our home. I quickly converted his leftover boards, wood scraps, and old doors from those jobs to my own projects. My love for tools and woodworking continually evolved, and I eventually became a home remodeler and builder.
>
> A few years ago, I decided that my youngest daughter, Amy, should have a playhouse of her own. My two older children, already in their early teens, didn't seem too interested, but they did lend a hand in the construction and painting.
>
> The biggest joke of the whole project was the anticipated timetable of the project. I'm used to building 5,000-square-foot custom homes in less than six months, so this little playhouse should have been a piece-of-cake project taking one weekend, right? Wrong! Because it was up in the air, it took several thousand trips up and down a ladder to make all the cuts. After eight weekends, the playhouse was completed. I used T1-11 plywood siding over standard construction framing. This was built on pressure-treated 4×4 posts anchored in concrete. I used the same paint and shingle colors to match our house and garage.

> The idea of the plank was to keep most adults out and to give the playhouse a tree-house effect, and it has been a real focal point for Amy and her friends. One of my clients has asked me to build one just like it for his home."

— *Don Cook*

GLOSSARY

barn sash: An inexpensive wood-frame window with one, four, or six panes, used for sheds or barns. They are perfect for clubhouses.

beam: A horizontal piece of wood that supports some part of a house or structure.

blocks or blocking: Short lengths of 2×4 that are used to hold in windows or doors, to strengthen the frame, or to provide something to nail to.

board-and-bat: A type of siding where wide boards are applied vertically to the house framing. The bats (short for battens) are narrow boards or wooden strips that are then nailed over the joints of the wide boards.

braces or bracing: Temporary boards that hold wall framing in place once it has been *plumbed.*

butt: The bottom edge of a shingle or clapboard.

car siding: Also known as rustic plank or V rustic siding. Pine boards 6″ to 8″ wide that are tongue-and-grooved and suitable for interior or exterior paneling or siding. Originally used for lining the inside walls of railway freight cars.

centerline: A mark to show where the middle of a board should be placed or nailed.

clapboards: Also known as beveled or lap siding. Long, narrow boards made of pine, redwood, or cedar that are thicker at one edge than the other. Clapboards are applied horizontally and overlapped to cover the outer walls of a wood-framed house.

coated sinker: A common steel nail that comes in sizes from about 1″ long (3d) to 3½″ long (16d). It is coated with a lubricant that allows the nail to be easily driven in but then immediately turns sticky to hold the nail tight in the wood.

cripple: A short stud below or above a window or door.

drywall: Also called Sheetrock, gypsum board, or wallboard. A common interior wall panel made of gypsum, a fireproof plasterlike mineral, and covered with heavy paper. Drywall is screwed or nailed to the *studs* and then can be plastered, painted, wallpapered, etc.

duplex nail: A common steel nail with two heads, used for temporary *bracing.* When the first head is all the way in, the second head is still far enough out to allow the nail to be pulled out again.

flush: Having surfaces on the same plane; even.

footprint: The area of ground a structure covers or occupies, usually described in square feet.

frame or framing: *(noun)* The wooden skeleton of a house made up of *studs, joists, rafters,* etc. *(verb)* To assemble the frame of a house or other structure.

furring strips: Pieces of pine, usually sold in 8-foot lengths, that are used to hold tiles, panels, or wallboard to the house frame. Furring strips are usually cheaper than "normal" lumber but of similar quality.

header: A beam that supports the wall or roof above a door or window.

jamb: The frame enclosing a door or a window.

joists: Boards laid parallel to each other and extending from wall to wall to support the floor or ceiling. Joists are usually laid 16″ or 24″ on center, meaning 16″ or 24″ from the center of one joist to the center of the next.

level: The condition of being perfectly flat, which can be tested with the tool that is also called a level.

lumber: Pieces of wood that are sawn from the logs of pine, fir, hemlock, cedar, or redwood trees. Lumber mills near forests saw the logs into standard-size boards that are then graded and sold through lumberyards and home centers.

nailer: An extra *stud*, *rafter*, or *joist* that provides a surface on which to nail *sheathing*, *siding*, *paneling*, or *drywall*.

oriented strand board (OSB) or waferboard: An inexpensive 4-foot by 8-foot panel made of wood chips (strands or wafers) laid down in a random (oriented) pattern, then glued and pressed together under tons of pressure. This material is used for *sheathing* or *siding* on houses all over the world.

paneling: Any thin plywood, fiberboard sheet, or boards used to finish an interior wall.

partition: An interior wall that divides a large room into smaller rooms.

paver: Any brick, stone, or concrete block used for walkways, patios, or driveways. Pavers come in a variety of colors, shapes, and sizes.

pier: A masonry (brick or concrete) column that holds up a main *beam* or a *sill* under the first floor.

pier block: A specially shaped concrete block with a wide bottom and narrow top used to hold up a foundation post or *sill*.

pilot hole: A hole drilled or poked into wood to accommodate or guide a screw. The pilot hole is slightly narrower than the shaft of the screw to allow the screw to "bite" the wood.

pitch: The steepness of a roof. A 1:12 pitch is almost flat; a 4:12 pitch is steeper, but you can still walk on it; and a 12:12 pitch is very steep.

plate: The top or bottom board that holds all the *studs* together in a wall frame. The top one is called the top plate, and the bottom one is usually called the bottom plate, but also the sole plate, bed plate, or shoe.

plumb: The condition of being exactly vertical, or straight up and down, which can be tested with a level or a *plumb bob*.

plumb bob: A pointed, conical-shaped weight held at the end of a string to test a wall or a post for *plumb*, or straight up and down.

pressure-treated: Wood that has had preservative chemicals forced into the grain under high pressure. Pressure-treated wood is used mostly for decking, fence posts, landscaping, and other places where it gets rained on or touches the ground.

rafters: Sloping boards laid parallel to each other to frame or support a roof.

rim joists: Joists that are set on the edge, or rim, of the foundation and run perpendicular to the floor joists.

sheathing: The structural exterior covering of a building, usually consisting of boards, plywood, or *oriented strand board*, that often adds to the building's strength and is then painted or covered with *siding.*

shim: A tapered, shinglelike wedge of wood used to level some part of a structure or to fill in a gap to hold something in place.

siding: Any exterior covering on a building, usually applied over *sheathing.* Common wood siding materials are *clapboards,* shingles, *board-and-bat,* and *T1-11 plywood.* Other common materials are vinyl siding, aluminum siding, fiber-cement board, brick, stone, and *stucco.*

sill: The beam or flat board laid on posts, piers, or the foundation wall that in turn supports the entire building.

square: A building is square when all the corners are at right angles, or 90°. This includes any rectangular or square-shaped room or building. A square foundation will make the rest of the building much easier to build.

stucco: An exterior plaster made of Portland cement, sand, and water, with acrylic binder and fiberglass sometimes added. Stucco is usually applied over a plastic or metal mesh lath.

stud: An upright post in the *frame* of a wall. Studs support the *siding* on the exterior and the *drywall* or *paneling* on the interior, and they also support the roof or upper stories. Studs are usually 2×4s or 2×6s.

T1-11 plywood: Plywood siding that also serves as structural sheathing. The sheets are smooth or have grooves every 4″, 8″, or 12″ for a design effect.

toenailing: A method of nailing thick boards together at an angle. (See the illustration on page 60.)

tongue-and-groove: An interlocking system that holds boards tightly together. Each board has a "tongue" on one edge that fits into the groove of its neighbor, so that together they can take a lot of stress, such as in the floor of a basketball court.

trimmer: A block attached to the stud adjoining a window or door to strengthen the framing.

INDEX

Acknowledgments

I deeply appreciate all the help of Deborah Balmuth, Nancy Ringer, Ilona Sherratt, and the rest of the staff at Storey Publishing in making this book a wonderful experience for me. It has been fun all the way!

Other Storey Titles You Will Enjoy

Catch the Wind, Harness the Sun, *by Michael J. Caduto.*
Introduce kids to renewable energy with these exciting activities and
experiments.
224 pages. Paper. ISBN 978-1-60342-794-4.
Hardcover. 978-1-60342-971-9.

Compact Cabins, *by Gerald Rowan.*
Simple living in 1,000 square feet or less — includes 62 design interpretations
for every taste.
216 pages. Paper. ISBN 978-1-60342-462-2.

The Kids' Building Workshop, *by J. Craig & Barbara Robertson.*
Easy projects to teach essential skills and build 15 fun and useful items.
144 pages. Paper. ISBN 978-1-58017-488-6.

Rustic Retreats: A Build-It-Yourself Guide,
by David and Jeanie Stiles.
Illustrated, step-by-step instructions for more than 20 low-cost, sturdy, beautiful
outdoor structures.
160 pages. Paper. ISBN 978-1-58017-035-2.

The Vegetable Gardener's Book of Building Projects.
Simple-to-make projects, including cold frames, compost bins, planters, raised
beds, outdoor furniture, and more.
152 pages. Paper. ISBN 978-1-60342-526-1.

Woodworking FAQ, *by Spike Carlsen.*
Practical answers to common woodworking questions, plus insider tips on how to
be successful in every project.
304 pages. Paper with partially concealed wire-o. ISBN 978-1-60342-729-6.

These and other books from Storey Publishing are available
wherever quality books are sold or by calling 1-800-441-5700.
Visit us at *www.storey.com*.